Arctic Tern

Common Tern

Sandwich Tern

Lesser Black-backed Gull

Black-headed Gull

Common Gull

Herring Gull

Great Skua

Glaucous Gull

Fulmar

Great Black-backed Gull

Chough

Mediterranean Gull

Manx Shearwater

Arctic Skua

Kittiwake

Pomarine Skua

Black Guillemot

Puffin

Rock Dove

Razorbill

Guillemot

Coastal & Sea Birds

CW01045704

Shore Lark

Brent Goose

Scaup

Storm Petrel

Snow Bunting

Red-breasted Merganser

Shelduck

Common Scoter

ck Pipit

Velvet Scoter

Eider

Long-tailed Duck

Curlew

Turnstone

Knot

Sanderling

Shag

Redshank

Gannet

Grey Plover

Put a ✔ sticker next to the birds you have seen

Bar-tailed Godwit

Oystercatcher

Cormorant

Purple Sandpiper

Avocet

Dunlin

Ringed Plover

sex CM7 4SL Printed in Hong Kong Artist: Alan Harris

Coastal & Sea Birds

handbook

Coastal & Sea Birds handbook

Written by
Duncan Brewer

Illustrated by
Alan Harris

MILES KELLY
PUBLISHING

First published in 2003 by Miles Kelly Publishing Ltd,
Bardfield Centre, Great Bardfield, Essex, CM7 4SL

British Library Cataloguing-in-Publication Data
A catalogue record for this book is available from the
British Library

ISBN 1-84236-312-3

2 4 6 8 10 9 7 5 3 1

Project Manager: Kate Miles
Assistant: Carol Danenbergs
Design: Guy Rodgers
Production: Estela Godoy

Contact us by email: info@mileskelly.net
Website: www.mileskelly.net

Printed in China

Key

 Gulls, Terns and Skuas

 Choughs

 Doves

 Auks and Fulmars

 Gannets and Cormorants

 Waders

 Larks, Pipits and Buntings

 Ducks

 Storm Petrels

CONTENTS

HOW TO USE THIS BOOK

Here are a few notes on finding your way round the pages of your bird guide. Read them and get started!

Place your 'I've seen it!' sticker here

Birdspotting record

Questions to help you successfully identify birds

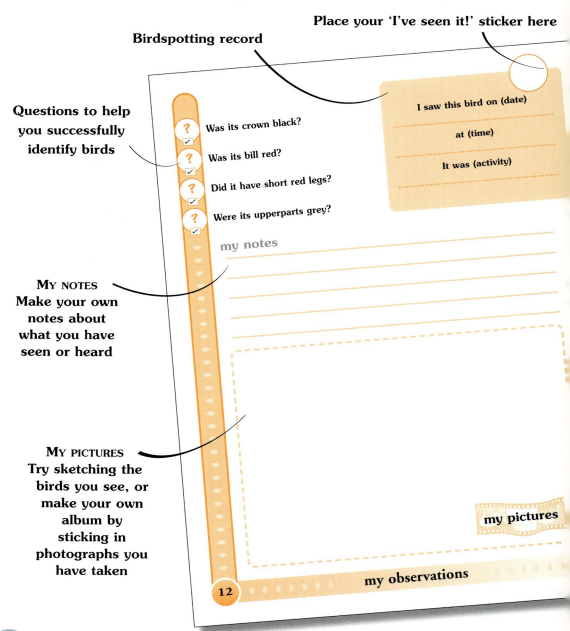

Was its crown black?

Was its bill red?

Did it have short red legs?

Were its upperparts grey?

my notes

I saw this bird on (date)

at (time)

It was (activity)

MY NOTES
Make your own notes about what you have seen or heard

MY PICTURES
Try sketching the birds you see, or make your own album by sticking in photographs you have taken

my pictures

my observations

12

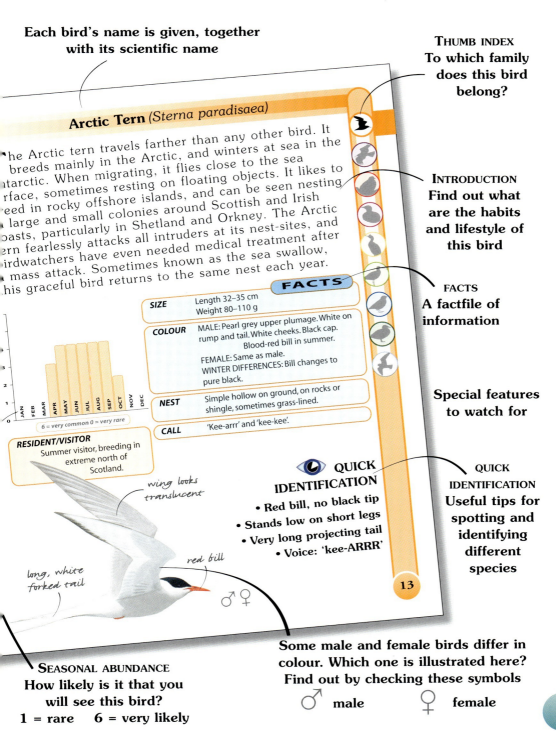

Each bird's name is given, together with its scientific name

THUMB INDEX
To which family does this bird belong?

Arctic Tern *(Sterna paradisaea)*

The Arctic tern travels farther than any other bird. It breeds mainly in the Arctic, and winters at sea in the Antarctic. When migrating, it flies close to the sea surface, sometimes resting on floating objects. It likes to breed in rocky offshore islands, and can be seen nesting in large and small colonies around Scottish and Irish coasts, particularly in Shetland and Orkney. The Arctic tern fearlessly attacks all intruders at its nest-sites, and birdwatchers have even needed medical treatment after a mass attack. Sometimes known as the sea swallow, this graceful bird returns to the same nest each year.

INTRODUCTION
Find out what are the habits and lifestyle of this bird

FACTS

SIZE	Length 32–35 cm Weight 80–110 g
COLOUR	MALE: Pearl grey upper plumage. White on rump and tail. White cheeks. Black cap. Blood-red bill in summer. FEMALE: Same as male. WINTER DIFFERENCES: Bill changes to pure black.
NEST	Simple hollow on ground, on rocks or shingle, sometimes grass-lined.
CALL	'Kee-arrr' and 'kee-kee'.

FACTS
A factfile of information

Special features to watch for

RESIDENT/VISITOR
Summer visitor, breeding in extreme north of Scotland.

6 = very common 0 = very rare

JAN FEB MAR APR MAY JUN JUL AUG SEP OCT NOV DEC

👁 QUICK IDENTIFICATION
• Red bill, no black tip
• Stands low on short legs
• Very long projecting tail
• Voice: 'kee-ARRR'

QUICK IDENTIFICATION
Useful tips for spotting and identifying different species

wing looks translucent

long, white forked tail

red bill

♂♀

SEASONAL ABUNDANCE
How likely is it that you will see this bird?
1 = rare   6 = very likely

Some male and female birds differ in colour. Which one is illustrated here? Find out by checking these symbols
♂ male   ♀ female

HOW TO IDENTIFY BIRDS

Watching sea birds on the coast or water birds in an estuary is enjoyable, but can be even more interesting once you learn their names. At first identifying a particular bird among a mixed crowd of squawking gulls might seem impossible. The secret is to learn how to look – and listen.

• A good way to start learning how to identify birds is to pick one bird and study it for as long as it remains in view, up to five minutes, say. You will need a notebook and pen, and binoculars could be a big help, but you do not need any other equipment. Choose your bird and make some notes. It may help to make a rough drawing.

• Note the bird's main body colour, and also note variations such as differently coloured head or wings. What colour are its beak and legs? What shape is its tail? Are its legs long or short?

• Nearly all seagulls and most other coastal birds like to congregate in flocks of their own kind. If you choose a bird from a flock, you can keep making notes from the same species even if the particular bird you are watching disappears.

• When you have noted as much as you can about its appearance, try and describe its calls. Add notes about the way it flies, how it behaves if it is feeding and what you think it is eating.

• Now briefly describe the habitat. Is it sitting on a cliff ledge, perching on a harbour wall, or wading through muddy shallows? Is it pulling worms out of the sand, diving for fish, or raiding dustbins? Habitat is very important when identifying nesting sea and coastal birds. You will have to learn which birds nest on cliff ledges, which nest on shingle, which in burrows or on marshy land.

Red-breasted Merganser

• Once you have described your bird to the best of your ability, it is time to check your bird guide. Can you recognize your bird from its picture and description?

• From now on, try to use the same terms as the guide for parts of a bird's body. Use 'cap' for the top of the head, 'nape' for the back of the neck and so on. The more you learn and use the correct terms, the better you can describe what you see.

• One problem, especially with sea birds, is that the young often have very different plumage from their parents despite being the same size. Often the young of different species look very similar. Watching which adults feed a young bird should help identification.

• When writing up your notes use headings such as colour, markings, habitat, shape, size, flight, call, etc. Also put the date, as birds often spend the seasons in different places.

The more you watch, the more you will see, and your identification will become more accurate. Before long you will be familiar with several species, and each birdwatching session will add knowledge and make you more confident in your fascinating new hobby.

On the rock face: 1.Great Black-backed gull 2.Lesser Black-headed gull 3. Herring gull 4. Rock Dove 5. Chough 6. Puffin 7. Guillemot 8. Razorbill 9. Rock Pipit 10. Fulmar 11. Kittiwake 12. Black Guillemot

HOW TO BIRDWATCH

Birdwatching is a rewarding and healthy activity. You learn not just about birds but about all aspects of the natural world, including other animals, plants, weather, the seasons and the landscape.

• All you need to start your birdwatching career is a notebook, a pencil, a bird guide, and the ability to sit still for ten minutes at a time. Large amounts of expensive weatherproof clothing are not essential. However, if you intend to watch birds at the coast, or elsewhere in the open, it is a good idea to have sensible footwear and a waterproof jacket. Wear enough layers to keep warm, and take a flask of hot drink and some food.

Puffin

• A pair of binoculars is likely to be your most expensive item of equipment. You can birdwatch without binoculars, but with them you can see small details that you would otherwise miss, and get a really close look at birds without scaring them. Binoculars usually have numbers on them, such as 8x30, or 9x40. The numbers give information about how big and how bright the binoculars make things look. A good size for general birdwatching is 8x30.

• If you have chosen a site to watch sea or coastal birds, it is a good idea to have an Ordnance Survey map of the area. This will help you find other likely sites within walking distance, and you can also use it to find your way back at the end of the day. It makes good sense to go birdwatching with friends or fellow club members. Take a torch in case you are caught in the dark. You should always leave details at home of where you intend to go and when you will be returning.

• On the coast many birdwatching sites include cliffs and rocky bays. Never attempt to climb cliffs to get closer to birds. Most cliffs are extremely dangerous, with loose rock, and sea birds are quite likely to attack anyone getting anywhere near their nests. You should never disturb a nest or take an egg. If you are down at sea level to watch birds, make sure you know what time the tide comes in and leave plenty of time to get clear.

• You will probably be taking notes to help you identify later, with the aid of your bird guide, what you see. A waterproof map case will keep your notes dry despite rain and spray.

Curlew

• Many birdwatchers take photographs of birds, but cameras with the right sort of telescopic lenses are very expensive, and your notes will probably give you a better idea of what you have been watching than a blurred photograph. There will be plenty of time later on, when you are more experienced, to consider buying cameras, tripods and any other natural history photographic equipment.

Arctic skua

Most of all, be patient, stay safe and enjoy the birds.

? ✓ Was its crown black?

? ✓ Was its bill red?

? ✓ Did it have short red legs?

? ✓ Were its upperparts grey?

I saw this bird on (date)

....

at (time)

....

It was (activity)

....

my notes

....

....

....

....

....

my pictures

Arctic Tern *(Sterna paradisaea)*

The Arctic tern travels farther than any other bird. It breeds mainly in the Arctic, and winters at sea in the Antarctic. When migrating, it flies close to the sea surface, sometimes resting on floating objects. It likes to breed in rocky offshore islands, and can be seen nesting in large and small colonies around Scottish and Irish coasts, particularly in Shetland and Orkney. The Arctic tern fearlessly attacks all intruders at its nest-sites, and birdwatchers have even needed medical treatment after a mass attack. Sometimes known as the sea swallow, this graceful bird returns to the same nest each year.

6 = very common 0 = very rare

RESIDENT/VISITOR
Summer visitor, breeding in extreme north of Scotland.

FACTS

SIZE	Length 32–35 cm Weight 80–110 g
COLOUR	MALE: Pearl grey upper plumage. White on rump and tail. White cheeks. Black cap. Blood-red bill in summer. FEMALE: Same as male. WINTER DIFFERENCES: Bill changes to pure black.
NEST	Simple hollow on ground, on rocks or shingle, sometimes grass-lined.
CALL	'Kee-arrr' and 'kee-kee'.

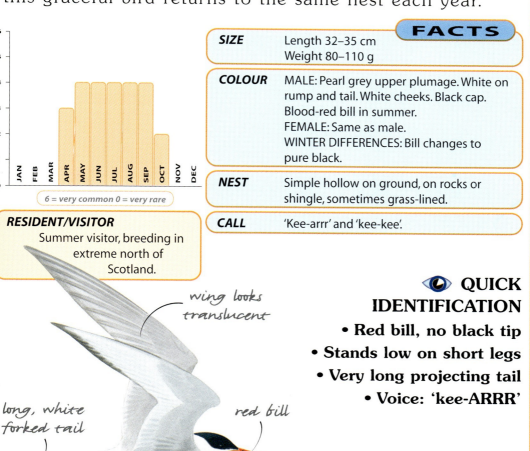

wing looks translucent

long, white forked tail

red bill

♂♀

👁 QUICK IDENTIFICATION
- **Red bill, no black tip**
- **Stands low on short legs**
- **Very long projecting tail**
- **Voice: 'kee-ARRR'**

? ✓ Was its beak short and thin?

? ✓ Did its beak have a black tip?

? ✓ Were its upperparts grey?

? ✓ Did it have a black crown?

I saw this bird on (date)

....

at (time)

....

It was (activity)

....

my notes

....

....

....

....

....

my pictures

my observations

Common Tern (Sterna hirundo)

The common tern is often seen over rivers, hovering and swooping as it feeds. Elegant and aggressive, it is the most abundant tern seen in Britain. It nests in noisy colonies, on beaches, sand-dunes and islands. Colonies sometimes all take off at once, in silence, and fly over the sea before returning to the nest-sites. It is not a good swimmer, and walks awkwardly on the ground because of its relatively short legs. It is light and graceful in flight, with rapid direction changes. The common tern may live as long as ten years.

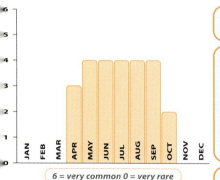

6 = very common 0 = very rare

RESIDENT/VISITOR
Visitor, arrives April and leaves October.

FACTS

SIZE	Length 32–33 cm Weight 100–140 g
COLOUR	MALE: Pale grey undersides. Pearl grey mantle. Dark grey band on wing undersides. Orange bill with black tip. FEMALE: Same as male. WINTER DIFFERENCES: Some black goes from forehead. White marks on upperwing surfaces. Bill turns black with red base.
NEST	A hollow on the ground. Island sites popular. In colonies.
CALL	High-pitched 'KEE-yah', and 'kik-ik-ik-ik'.

QUICK IDENTIFICATION

- **Dark band at back edge of wing undersides**
- **Orange bill with black tip**
- **Whiter undersides than Arctic tern**
- **Tail streamers no longer than closed wings**

♂ ♀

inner wing feathers translucent

grey back

black tip to red bill

15

? ☑ Did it have a black and white forehead?

? ☑ Was its bill yellow with a black tip?

? ☑ Were its legs yellow?

? ☑ Was it small and fast-flying?

I saw this bird on (date)

....

at (time)

....

It was (activity)

....

my notes

my pictures

my observations

Little Tern (Sterna albifrons)

The little tern is tiny compared to the other British terns. It nests on shingle ridges and sandy beaches, which brings it into conflict with holidaymakers. Like other terns it hovers and dives when fishing, and uses very fast wing beats, which give it a flickering flight. It can often be seen fishing right above the waves as they break on the beach. It dives for surface fish, but also catches insects on the wing. Its breeding colonies are small, and it flies around intruders repeating a 'duip' alarm call, then falling back until the coast is clear.

FACTS

SIZE	Length 25 cm Weight 50–60 g
COLOUR	MALE: Pale grey upperparts and wings. Rump and tail white. Black front edge to wings. Black cap and white forehead. Black stripe from eye. Yellow bill with black tip. FEMALE: Duller bill, feet and legs. WINTER DIFFERENCES: Crown mottled.
NEST	On ground in sand or shingle.
CALL	Fast 'kirri-ki-ki' and 'kyik'.

6 = very common 0 = very rare

RESIDENT/VISITOR
Summer visitor, arriving April and leaving by September for West African coast.

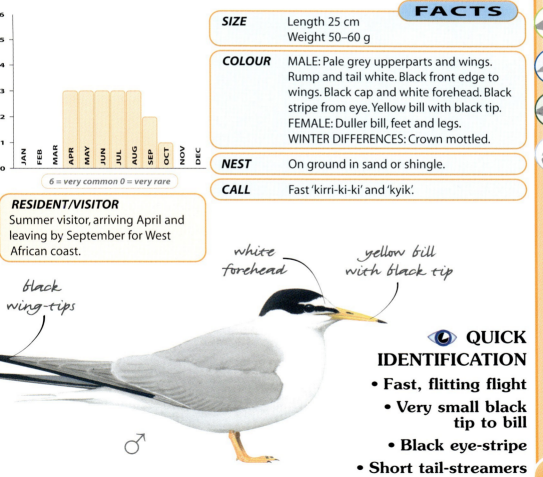

black wing-tips

white forehead

yellow bill with black tip

♂

QUICK IDENTIFICATION

- Fast, flitting flight
- Very small black tip to bill
- Black eye-stripe
- Short tail-streamers

17

? ✓ Was it quite a large bird?

? ✓ Was its black cap ragged at the back?

? ✓ Were its legs black?

? ✓ Was its bill black with a yellow tip?

I saw this bird on (date)

....

at (time)

....

It was (activity)

....

my notes

my pictures

my observations

Sandwich Tern *(Sterna sandvicensis)*

This is the largest of the terns visiting the British Isles. It is the first to arrive in the spring, and many pairs breed on shingle beaches, in coastal dunes, and around some inland waters. The noise of a large colony can be heard a considerable distance away. The sandwich tern likes being in large groups, and often mixes with other terns. It dives from a greater height than most terns when fishing and disappears entirely under water. It is also less aggressive towards intruders. It still swoops down but does not strike. It lives on sand-eels, fish and molluscs. Once the young have left the nest, they may be fed by any of the adults in the group.

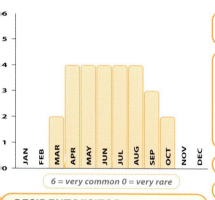

6 = very common 0 = very rare

FACTS

SIZE	Length 36–38 cm Weight 210–250 g
COLOUR	MALE: Pearl-grey mantle. White, sometimes pinkish underparts. Long black bill with small yellow tip. Black forehead, crown and nape. FEMALE: Same as male. WINTER DIFFERENCES: Forehead white. Crown and nape speckled with grey.
NEST	Scraped hollow on ground. In colonies.
CALL	Loud 'kirrik' and 'kik'.

RESIDENT/VISITOR
Visitor, arrives late March, departs October.

👁 QUICK IDENTIFICATION

- **Large size, short forked tail**
- **Long black bill, yellow-tipped**
- **Shaggy crest at back of head when excited or sleeping**
- **Long wings and somewhat gull-like flight**

black crown

white rump

white breast

♂ ♀

? ✓ Was its flight gliding and soaring?

? ✓ If seen in summer, was its head dark brown?

? ✓ Was its outer underwing dark?

? ✓ Did it have a raucous call?

I saw this bird on (date)

....

at (time)

....

It was (activity)

....

my notes

my pictures

Black-headed Gull (*Larus ridibundus*)

One of the commonest British gulls, the black-headed gull is now found inland, both feeding and breeding, as often as on the shore. In its coastal habitat of low shores, harbours and estuaries, fish is an important part of its diet. However, its increased presence inland owes much to its enthusiasm for garbage dumps and the worms which surface from playing fields. Inland it feeds on insects, worms and snails as well as waste scraps and carrion. Black-headed gulls are often seen following a plough. They are fond of swimming, and outside the breeding season sometimes come into riverside cities.

6 = very common 0 = very rare

RESIDENT/VISITOR
Resident, but numbers swelled in winter by continental visitors.

FACTS

SIZE	Length 35–38 cm Weight 230–260 g
COLOUR	MALE: White neck, breast, underparts and back. Blue-grey wings. Chocolate-brown head in spring. Black wing-tips. White leading edge to wings. FEMALE: Same as male. WINTER DIFFERENCES: White head, with dark 'ear' spot.
NEST	Grass and sticks, in marshes, sand-hills, lake islands, shingle. In colonies.
CALL	'Kwarr' and 'kwwup', plus a raucous scream. Long, squealing calls.

red bill

incomplete eye-ring

👁 QUICK IDENTIFICATION

- **Dark head in spring and summer**
- **Small size, slim shape**
- **Deep red bill and legs**
- **White leading edge to wings**

long, red legs

♂ ♀

? ✓ Was its bill yellowish in colour?

? ✓ Were its wing-tips black with white markings?

? ✓ Was its breast white?

? ✓ Was its back grey?

I saw this bird on (date)

....

at (time)

....

It was (activity)

....

my notes

_____

_____

_____

_____

_____

my pictures

Common Gull *(Larus canus)*

Far less common in England and Wales than its name suggests, the common gull is more numerous in Scotland, particularly in the north and the islands. It is a good swimmer and diver, and will submerge entirely in pursuit of fish. It is increasingly seen inland, usually in farming areas, and also around reservoirs and lakes. It is a scavenger which will eat most things, including bird eggs. Common gulls are social birds, and will gang up on a predator such as a hawk or a skua threatening the community.

Chart (months JAN–DEC, scale 0–6):
6 = very common 0 = very rare

RESIDENT/VISITOR
Resident in the north, but a winter visitor in the south.

FACTS

SIZE	Length 40–42 cm Weight 350–450 g
COLOUR	MALE: Pale grey upperparts. White underparts. Black and white patches at wing-tips. Green-yellow bill and yellowy legs. FEMALE: Same as male. WINTER DIFFERENCES: Grey-brown streaks on head and breast.
NEST	Bulky, of grass, seaweed, heather and moss. On ground or ledge.
CALL	High, shrill, squealing yelps and chattering cries.

👁 QUICK IDENTIFICATION

- **Greenish yellow legs and bill**
- **Dark eye**
- **Small and non-aggressive**
- **Slender shape**

rounded head

light grey back

slender body and legs

♂ ♀

? Did it have a pale grey back? ✓

? Did it have a yellow bill with a red spot? ✓

? Was it a large bird? ✓

? Did it have a large head? ✓

I saw this bird on (date)

at (time)

It was (activity)

my notes

my pictures

my observations

Glaucous Gull *(Larus hyperboreus)*

The large glaucous gull is fairly rare in Britain. It visits in winter from its Arctic breeding-grounds, and is most often seen in groups of mixed gulls. They appear inland on reservoirs and scavenging in refuse tips. The glaucous gull is fond of crabs and shellfish, and hangs around fish docks with other gulls on the look-out for fish scraps. It is a bold bird, and feared by smaller gulls, but is not as aggressive as the greater black-backed gull. It takes other birds' eggs, and will also catch small mammals if given the chance. As well as eating animal food, it is known to feed on plants, including seaweed and berries.

6 = very common 0 = very rare

FACTS

SIZE	Length 62–68 cm Weight 1500–2200 g
COLOUR	MALE: Silver-grey mantle. Pure white elsewhere. Yellow bill with red spot. FEMALE: Same as male. WINTER DIFFERENCES: Head streaked with brown.
NEST	Moss and seaweed, above and below sea-cliffs in colonies on Arctic islands. Not in Britain.
CALL	Almost silent in winter. Occasional 'eeee-yoch-yoch-yoch' and 'kak-ak-ak'.

RESIDENT/VISITOR
Autumn and winter visitor from the Arctic, usually to east coast.

white wing-tips

red spot on bill

♂ ♀

pink legs

 QUICK IDENTIFICATION

- **No black on tail or wings**
- **Large size and heavy bill**
- **Lemon yellow eye-ring**
- **Slow wing-beats in flight**

25

? ☑ Was it a large bird?

? ☑ Did it have a red spot on its thick, yellow bill?

? ☑ Were its legs pale pinkish?

? ☑ Was its back black?

I saw this bird on (date)

at (time)

It was (activity)

my notes

my pictures

Great Black-backed Gull *(Larus marinus)*

The great black-backed gull is an imposing bird, dramatically coloured, bulky and equipped with a powerful beak. It usually lives around rocky coasts and cliffs, though it is increasingly found in estuaries, and inland at reservoirs, tips and fields. It is a fearsome predator as well as a scavenger. It can gulp down a whole rabbit, and will attack flocks of water birds in search of a meal. It also hangs around docks and fishing boats, especially in winter. The great black-backed gull can soar to great heights, and also skims the waves, like an albatross. It feeds on carrion when it gets the chance, and one of its local names is corpse-eater.

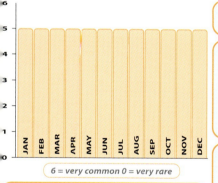

JAN FEB MAR APR MAY JUN JUL AUG SEP OCT NOV DEC

6 = very common 0 = very rare

RESIDENT/VISITOR
Resident, with many over-wintering visitors.

FACTS

SIZE	Length 62–65 cm Weight 1500–2000 g
COLOUR	MALE: Black mantle and wings. White head and body. White wing-tip spots. Bill yellow with red spot. FEMALE: Same colouring, but smaller, with smaller head and bill. WINTER DIFFERENCES: Dark streaks on head.
NEST	Large, of heather, sticks, lined with grass or seaweed. In a cliff-top hollow. Occasionally on moors.
CALL	Deep-pitched 'owk-uk-uk-uk'. Also wails and squeals.

👁 QUICK IDENTIFICATION

- **Deep black back and upperwings**
- **Great size and bulk**
- **White wing-spots visible in flight**
- **Heavy, deep bill**

big head and bill

black back

white breast

? ✓ Were its grey wings tipped with black?

? ✓ Was its flight strong and powerful?

? ✓ Did you see it near the land?

? ✓ Was its call loud?

I saw this bird on (date)

at (time)

It was (activity)

my notes

my pictures

my observations

Herring Gull (*Larus argentatus*)

The most widespread of our coastal gulls, the herring gull is well known to holidaymakers at seaside towns and beaches. It has even taken to nesting on rooftops in resorts. It swiftly becomes tame, especially if fed. It has developed many feeding strategies, such as trampling the ground to make worms come to the surface, and dropping crabs and shellfish onto rocks or tarmac to break them open. The herring gull is very skilful in flight, and follows fishing boats, gliding and riding the wind as it waits for fish scraps to be thrown overboard. In the winter it can sometimes be seen resting in flocks on fields and reservoirs.

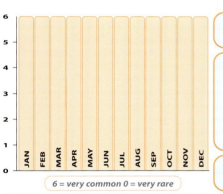

	JAN	FEB	MAR	APR	MAY	JUN	JUL	AUG	SEP	OCT	NOV	DEC

6 = very common 0 = very rare

RESIDENT/VISITOR
Resident, with many autumn/winter visitors from the continent.

FACTS

SIZE	Length 52–55 cm Weight 750–1200 g
COLOUR	MALE: Pale grey upperparts. White head, neck and underparts. Black and white wing-tips. Yellow bill with red spot. FEMALE: Same as male. WINTER DIFFERENCES: Dark streaks on head and breast. All plumage dirty-white.
NEST	Untidy structure of available materials, including heather, seaweed and grasses.
CALL	'Kyow' repeated, and 'ga-ga-ga' when anxious.

♂ ♀

pale iris

yellow bill
with red spot

grey wings

white
underparts

👁 QUICK IDENTIFICATION

- **Pink legs**
- **Much larger than similar common gull**
- **Heavy, hooked yellow bill with red spot**
- **Bold around humans**

? ☑ Was its crown white?

? ☑ Was its back all a dark colour?

? ☑ Were its legs yellow?

? ☑ Was its bill yellow with a red spot?

I saw this bird on (date)
....

at (time)
....

It was (activity)
....

my notes
....
....
....
....

my pictures

my observations

Lesser Black-backed Gull *(Larus fuscus)*

Abird of islands, moors and cliff-tops, the lesser black-backed gull is a fierce predator of other sea birds, as well as of their eggs and young. It follows fishing boats and other vessels far out to sea, much farther than most other birds, often for many hours at a time. It also scavenges harbours and dumps. It is very protective of its nest and young, and a whole colony will take to the air to drive off intruders. The chicks leave the nest a few days after hatching, and forage on the ground, guarded by their parents for at least six weeks.

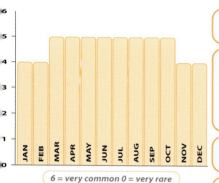

6 = very common 0 = very rare

RESIDENT/VISITOR
Summer breeding visitor, arriving in February, and leaving for Portugal and North Africa in November. Some birds over winter in Britain.

FACTS

SIZE	Length 50–52 cm Weight 600–1000 g
COLOUR	MALE: Slate-grey wing backs. Black wing-tips with white spots. FEMALE: Same as male. WINTER DIFFERENCES: Grey-brown head and dull yellow legs.
NEST	On the ground, in colonies. Heather stalks and seaweed.
CALL	Loud, deep 'ow-ow-ow-kyow'.

QUICK IDENTIFICATION

- **Much smaller than similar great black-backed gull**
- **Bright yellow legs and feet**
- **Dark primary wing feathers seen when flying**
- **Long wings, short legs compared to herring gull**

thick bill shape

all dark upperparts

yellow legs

white marks on wing-tips

♂ ♀

? ✓ Was its bill red and droopy shaped?

? ✓ In summer, was its head black?

? ✓ Were its legs red?

? ✓ Were its back and wings pale grey?

I saw this bird on (date)

at (time)

It was (activity)

my notes

my pictures

my observations

Mediterranean Gull (*Larus melanocephalus*)

Rare in Britain, but increasing in numbers, the Mediterranean gull can sometimes be found around western and southern coasts in marshes and coastal flat lands. Closely related to the British black-headed gull, the Mediterranean gull is a bulkier bird, with a heavier bill and longer legs. It feeds mainly on insects, crabs and small fish. It usually breeds in the Balkans and southeastern Europe, but up to 50 pairs now breed annually in the British Isles, in salt marshes and tidal mud flats. It may fly great distances from the colony to feed on grasslands, and also likes to feed at the edge of the sea close to breaking waves.

	JAN	FEB	MAR	APR	MAY	JUN	JUL	AUG	SEP	OCT	NOV	DEC

6 = very common 0 = very rare

RESIDENT/VISITOR
Mainly a spring visitor, though some pairs spend the winter and nest.

FACTS

SIZE	Length 36–38 cm. Weight 300–400 g
COLOUR	MALE: Pearl-grey upperwings. White underwings. Black hood. Red bill. FEMALE: Same as male. WINTER DIFFERENCES: Dusky face, dark bill. Dark smudge around and behind eye.
NEST	On ground near water, in colonies. Rare in Britain.
CALL	'Keeow' and 'ayeeah'. When alarmed 'ga-ga-ga'.

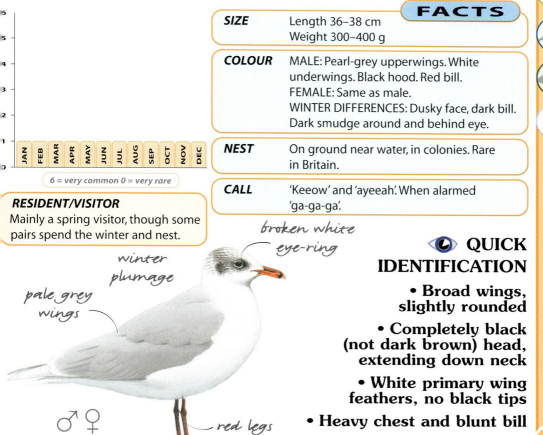

winter plumage

broken white eye-ring

pale grey wings

♂♀

red legs

QUICK IDENTIFICATION

- **Broad wings, slightly rounded**
- **Completely black (not dark brown) head, extending down neck**
- **White primary wing feathers, no black tips**
- **Heavy chest and blunt bill**

? ✓ Was its throat yellowish?

? ✓ Did it have a thin, short, black bill?

? ✓ Was its belly white?

? ✓ Did it have a high voice?

I saw this bird on (date)

....

at (time)

....

It was (activity)

....

my notes

_____

_____

_____

_____

_____

my pictures

my observations

Arctic Skua *(Stercorarius parasiticus)*

The fast and acrobatic Arctic skua relentlessly chases puffins, kittiwakes and terns to make them bring up fish they have eaten, which it then catches and eats in midair. During the chase it sprints and turns like a hawk. Its normal flight is steady and graceful. The Arctic skua's attacks on terns are particularly successful. When protecting its nest and young, it will attack anything from sheep to humans. The colony usually posts two or three sentry birds to give the alarm when predators or other intruders approach. As well as fish, the Arctic tern kills and eats adult and young birds, and will also feed on carrion.

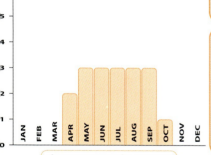

6 = very common 0 = very rare

FACTS

SIZE	Length 41–46 cm Weight 350–550 g
COLOUR	MALE: Two forms. Light form – blackish crown, dark upperparts, yellowish neck and sides of face, white underparts, dark breast band. Dark form – blackish brown all over, with slightly paler underparts. FEMALE: Same as male. WINTER DIFFERENCES: Light form becomes barred above and below.
NEST	On ground on moors, in colonies.
CALL	Wails, barks and a squealing 'eee-air'.

RESIDENT/VISITOR
Summer breeding visitor to northern Scotland and islands. Arrives late April, departs late October. Offshore migrant on most British coasts in autumn.

👁 QUICK IDENTIFICATION

- **Straight and pointed central tail spike**
- **Hawkish behaviour, harassing terns and puffins**
- **Hooked bill**
- **Pale wing-flashes when flying**

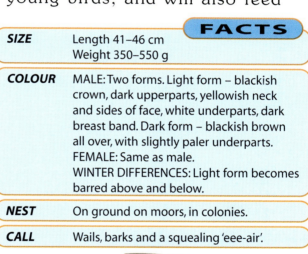

tail feathers long and twisted

♂ ♀

white wing-flash

? ✓ Did it look like a big brown gull?

? ✓ Were its legs brown?

? ✓ Did it have white wing-flashes?

? ✓ Did it have a small bill and head?

I saw this bird on (date)

....

at (time)

....

It was (activity)

....

my notes

my pictures

my observations

Great Skua *(Stercorarius skua)*

The bulky great skua chases birds to steal their meals as other skuas do, but goes for large prey, such as gannets, gulls and ducks. In the summer it also kills and eats other sea birds. It brings down its prey by dive-bombing it from a great height. Once almost extinct in the British Isles, the great skua has made a comeback, and is a regular summer resident in northern sites in the Orkney and Shetland islands. It is rarely seen inland in winter. It makes alarming attacks on intruders to its nest-sites, swooping down in a steep dive and striking with its feet as it sweeps past.

6 = very common 0 = very rare

FACTS

SIZE	Length 53–58 cm Weight 1300–2000 g
COLOUR	MALE: Dark brown speckled plumage. Darker cap. Dark wings with conspicuous white underwing patches. Rusty brown underparts. Black legs and bill. FEMALE: Same as male. WINTER DIFFERENCES: None.
NEST	On ground near sea in colonies.
CALL	Harsh 'skeerr', also 'tuh-tuh' when attacking.

RESIDENT/VISITOR
Breeding visitor to northern islands in summer. Migrates south for West Africa, mid-Atlantic and South America in winter.

👁 QUICK IDENTIFICATION

- **Large pale wing-patches visible at a distance**
- **Bulky shape**
- **Broad wings, slightly rounded**
- **Short tail, no projections**

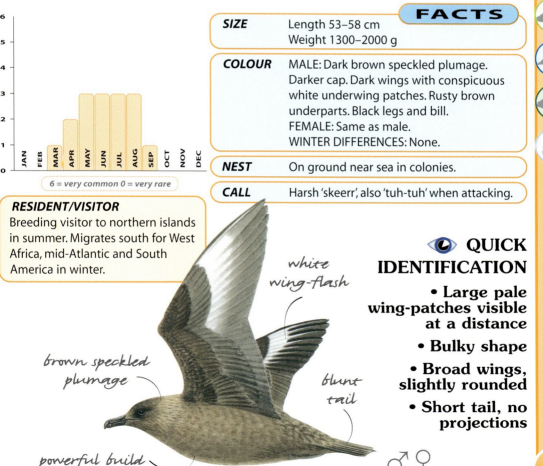

white wing-flash

brown speckled plumage

blunt tail

powerful build

♂ ♀

? ✓ Was its tail black with long central feathers?

? ✓ Was its throat yellowish?

? ✓ Was there a smudgy band on its breast?

? ✓ Did it look gull-like?

I saw this bird on (date)

....

at (time)

....

It was (activity)

....

my notes

my pictures

my observations

Pomarine Skua *(Stercorarius pomarinus)*

A fish-pirate like other skuas, the pomarine skua is between the Arctic and great skuas in size, and is usually seen far out to sea off eastern and southern English coasts. It is occasionally seen inland after a storm. It is a fast and agile flier using its skills in the air to chase birds such as herring and lesser black-backed gulls, sometimes forcing them down into the sea. In the Arctic, lemmings make up a major part of its diet. It also feeds on fish at sea, and on ships' refuse. It breeds in northern Europe, Asia, North America and Greenland.

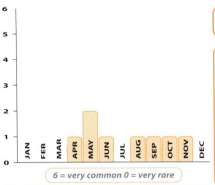

6 = very common 0 = very rare

FACTS

SIZE	Length 50-52 cm Weight 700 g
COLOUR	MALE: Two forms. Light form – dark upperparts and breast band, light underparts, white wing-flashes, blackish head and crown, yellowish over ears and back of neck. Dark form – blackish brown all over, underparts slightly paler. FEMALE: Same as male. WINTER DIFFERENCES: No colour differences. Shorter tail spike, untwisted.
NEST	Depression in moss in swampy Arctic tundra. Not in Britain.
CALL	'Which-yew'.

RESIDENT/VISITOR
Winter visitor offshore. Spring and autumn passage migrant.

👁 QUICK IDENTIFICATION

- Long, twisted, spoon-like tail feathers
- Yellowish brown hooked bill
- Wings broad at base
- Stouter, deeper-chested than Arctic skua; similar colouring

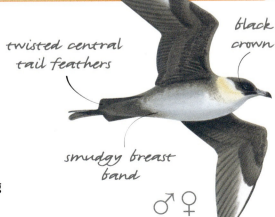

twisted central tail feathers

black crown

smudgy breast band

♂ ♀

39

? ☑ Was it a crow-like bird?

? ☑ Was it black all over?

? ☑ Were its bill and legs red?

? ☑ Were its wings fingered at the tips?

I saw this bird on (date)

....

at (time)

....

It was (activity)

....

my notes

my pictures

my observations

Chough *(Pyrrhocorax pyrrhocorax)*

The chough is the rarest member of the crow family in Britain, and is easily distinguished from other crows. It is found along coastal cliffs, swooping along and calling loudly, and often flies in small flocks. It is particularly acrobatic during the spring nesting season, soaring and tumbling, and even turning upside down. The chough feeds inland of the cliffs on the fields where it nests. It eats insects and worms, as well as dropping down to sea level to eat little crabs and shellfish. It sometimes feeds on grain left in stubble after harvesting. In 2002, wild chicks hatched in Cornwall, where the chough is the county's official bird, for the first time in 50 years.

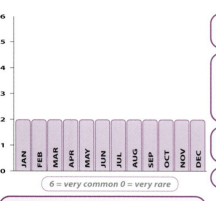

6 = very common 0 = very rare

RESIDENT/VISITOR
Resident.

FACTS

SIZE	Length 40 cm Weight 280–360 g
COLOUR	MALE: Glossy blue-black all over. Bill and legs red. FEMALE: Same as male. WINTER DIFFERENCES: None.
NEST	Simple hollow on ground, on rocks or shingle, sometimes grass-lined.
CALL	'Kweeow' or 'chee-ah'.

👁 QUICK IDENTIFICATION

- **Long, curved, red bill and red legs**
- **Coastal cliff habitat**
- **Distinctive call**
- **Aerobatic flight on very broad wings**

square-shaped tail

curved red bill

all black feathers

♂♀

41

? ☑ Was it pale grey with shiny neck patches?

? ☑ Did its folded wing show two black bars?

? ☑ Was its bill black-and-white?

? ☑ Were its legs pink?

I saw this bird on (date)

....

at (time)

....

It was (activity)

....

my notes

....

....

....

....

....

my pictures

my observations

Rock Dove (*Columba livia*)

The rock dove is the ancestor of all domestic pigeons. These were originally bred from wild birds for eating and for racing. The feral pigeons seen in both town and country are descendants of domestic escapees. In its natural state the rock dove lives among the rocks and cliffs of coasts and islands. It feeds on seeds and plant material in fields and woods, and perches on rocks or on the ground in preference to trees. Very few pure rock doves have survived in most parts of the country, due to interbreeding with feral relatives. Those that do remain breed on cliffs in northwestern Scotland and western Ireland.

6 = very common 0 = very rare

RESIDENT/VISITOR
Resident.

FACTS

SIZE	Length 31–34 cm Weight 250–350 g
COLOUR	MALE: Bluish body. Light grey back and wings. Double dark wing-bars. Metallic green and purple neck. White rump and underwing. FEMALE: Same as male. WINTER DIFFERENCES: None.
NEST	Roots, seaweed, heather on rocky ledge.
CALL	'Ruh-ruh-ruh'.

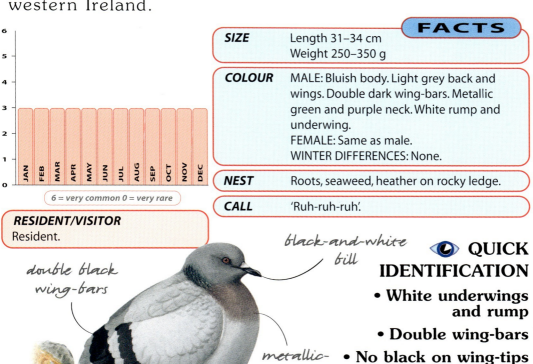

double black wing-bars

black-and-white bill

metallic-looking neck pattern

♂ ♀

👁 QUICK IDENTIFICATION

- **White underwings and rump**
- **Double wing-bars**
- **No black on wing-tips**
- **Flies low over water**

? ☑ Were its upperparts dark chocolate-brown in colour?

? ☑ Was its bill short, thin and pointed?

? ☑ Were its legs short and black?

? ☑ Was its breast white?

I saw this bird on (date)

....

at (time)

....

It was (activity)

....

my notes

my pictures

my observations

Guillemot (*Uria alge*)

The guillemot spends much of its life at sea, coming ashore to breed in packed colonies on cliff ledges and on the flat tops of off-shore rock stacks. Groups of guillemots fly up to 50 kilometres to their feeding-grounds each day. Their relatively short wings have a fast, whirring beat as they skim low over the water. The guillemot is a strong and expert swimmer, diving as deep as 50 metres in pursuit of fish. About three weeks after hatching, the guillemot chick leaps down from the cliffs to the water or rocks below, where it is joined by the male parent, which leads it out to sea.

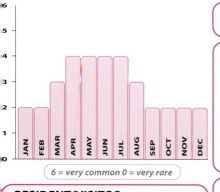

6 = very common 0 = very rare

RESIDENT/VISITOR
Resident.

FACTS

SIZE	Length 38–41 cm Weight 750–1000 g
COLOUR	MALE: Dark chocolate-brown head and upper body. White undersides, with brown streaks on flanks. So-called 'bridled' birds have a narrow white eye-ring extending into a line behind the eye. FEMALE: Same as male. WINTER DIFFERENCES: White chin, sides of head, neck. Dark line extends back from eye.
NEST	On cliff ledges, in dense colonies. Sometimes among boulders.
CALL	Extended 'aarrgh'.

👁 QUICK IDENTIFICATION

- **Dagger-like bill**
- **Dark chocolate-brown tinge to plumage**
- **Dark brown streaks in flanks**
- **Smaller and slimmer than razorbill**

blackish-brown plumage

white underparts

short rounded tail

♂ ♀

? ☑ Did its wings have white patches?

? ☑ Was the rest of its plumage black?

? ☑ Was the inside of its mouth bright red?

? ☑ Were its legs short and red?

I saw this bird on (date)

....

at (time)

....

It was (activity)

....

my notes

_____

_____

_____

_____

_____

my pictures

my observations

Black Guillemot *(Cepphus grylle)*

The black guillemot is about the size of a pigeon, and nests in small groups, not gathering like the guillemot in huge colonies. It flies fast and low, and can swim expertly under water, catching small fish and seabed creatures such as worms and molluscs. It is found around the coasts of Ireland and north and west Scotland, in Anglesey in Wales, and Cumbria in England. When threatening intruders it opens its beak very wide to reveal the bright red interior. It tends to stay closer to land than other guillemots, fishing in shallow waters. It winters at sea, not too far from its breeding territories, returning each year to the same nest site.

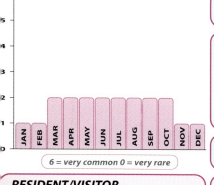

6 = very common 0 = very rare

RESIDENT/VISITOR
Resident.

FACTS	
SIZE	Length 30–32 cm Weight 340–450 g
COLOUR	MALE: Black plumage all over, except for large white wing-patches. Bright red feet. FEMALE: Same as male. WINTER DIFFERENCES: Whitish underparts and head, with pale barring. Wings barred deep grey and white. White patches remain.
NEST	Among boulders, in crevices on rocky shores and cliffs. Sometimes in old burrows.
CALL	Very high-pitched whistles and whines. 'Dinsie-dinsie'.

summer plumage all black

black bill

white wing-patch

♂ ♀

👁 QUICK IDENTIFICATION

- **Small size compared to guillemots**
- **Bright red feet**
- **Large white patches visible both sides of wings**
- **Bright red gape when calling or threatening**

? ✓ Did it have a yellow, short, stubby bill?

? ✓ Did it look gull-like?

? ✓ Were its legs yellow?

? ✓ Was it grey and white?

I saw this bird on (date)

....

at (time)

....

It was (activity)

....

my notes

my pictures

my observations

Fulmar (Fulmarus glacialis)

The fulmar is a true sea bird which never feeds on land. It can glide like an albatross on stiff wings over a metre wide, staying close to the sea surface. It is found all around the British coast, wherever there are cliffs for it to nest. The fulmar spends most of its time at sea, and is an enthusiastic follower of fishing boats. A large increase in British fulmar numbers in the 20th century may have been due to plentiful supplies of fish waste and offal from trawlers and whalers. Fulmars defend their nests energetically, and may eject a foul-smelling 'fulmar oil' at persistent intruders.

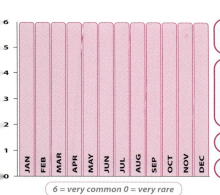

6 = very common 0 = very rare

RESIDENT/VISITOR
Resident.

FACTS

SIZE	Length 45–50 cm Weight 750 g
COLOUR	MALE: White head and underparts. Brownish-grey upperwings and body. FEMALE: Same as male. WINTER DIFFERENCES: None.
NEST	On cliff ledges in colonies.
CALL	Cackling 'ag-ag-ag-arrr'.

👁 QUICK IDENTIFICATION

- **Stiff-winged, banking, gliding flight**
- **Short, hooked bill with nostril tubes**
- **Wedge-shaped grey tail**
- **Fat cigar-shaped body**

yellow bill

grey upperparts

white breast

square, short tail

♂ ♀

? ☑ Did its call sound like its name (kitti-way-ake)?

? ☑ Did it have black legs?

? ☑ Was it white-breasted with grey wings?

? ☑ Did it have black wing-tips?

I saw this bird on (date)

....

at (time)

....

It was (activity)

....

my notes

....

....

....

....

....

my pictures

my observations

Kittiwake *(Rissa tridactyla)*

The kittiwake usually fishes on the surface of the sea, and never scavenges the tideline like other gulls. It feeds on fishes, crustaceans, worms and trawler wastes. The kittiwake is the smallest of the gulls breeding in the British Isles. It spends the winter at sea, and the spring and summer on some of the most inaccessible and sheer cliff-ledge nest-sites in the country. In flight the kittiwake is graceful, and it moves faster than larger gulls, using rapid wing-beats. It dives like a tern from the air when fishing, and uses its wings to swim under water.

6 = very common 0 = very rare

RESIDENT/VISITOR
Resident breeder, with a small number of winter visitors.

FACTS

SIZE	Length 38–41 cm Weight 350–440 g
COLOUR	MALE: Grey back. Black wing-tips. White head and body. Grenish yellow bill. FEMALE: Same as male. WINTER DIFFERENCES: Nape and crown greyer.
NEST	Seaweed, moss and grass, moulded with mud into a firm cup. On tiny ledges in crowded colonies.
CALL	'Kitti-way-ake'.

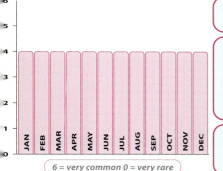

black wing-tips

grey back

white underparts

♂ ♀

👁 QUICK IDENTIFICATION

- **Distinctive 'kittiwake' call**
- **Black wing-tips**
- **Slender greenish-yellow bill**
- **Black three-toed feet**

? ✓ Did it have a parrot-like, colourful bill?

? ✓ Were its upperparts black?

? ✓ Did it have a white face?

? ✓ Were its legs short and red?

I saw this bird on (date)
....

at (time)
....

It was (activity)
....

my notes

_____

_____

_____

_____

_____

my pictures

my observations

Puffin (Fratercula arctica)

The puffin is unmistakable, with its black crown and colourful summer bill contrasting with its white face. It breeds in large colonies in Britain and Ireland. It is an accomplished diver and swimmer, frequently diving up to 15 metres, and is capable of catching several fish without surfacing. It holds them cross-wise in its large bill. Puffins choose the grassy slopes at the top of cliffs for their breeding-sites, and build their nests in burrows. They either excavate these themselves, or use old rabbit or shearwater burrows. Puffins have large, strong feet which they use as air-brakes when landing, as well as for swimming and burrow-digging.

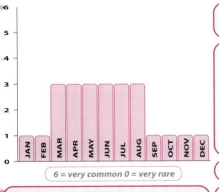

6 = very common 0 = very rare

RESIDENT/VISITOR
Resident.

FACTS

SIZE	Length 30 cm Weight 400 g
COLOUR	MALE: Black cap, neck and upperparts. White face. Bright red, yellow and blue bill. Red eye-ring. Small blue markings above and below eye. Orangey-red feet. FEMALE: Same as male. WINTER DIFFERENCES: Dark grey face, bill smaller and duller.
NEST	At the end of a burrow, up to 2 m deep.
CALL	A growling 'ka-arr-arr' in the colony.

👁 QUICK IDENTIFICATION

- **Parrot-like profile with brightly coloured bill**
- **Large orangey-red feet**
- **Gathers in 'rafts' of many birds on sea below colony**
- **Low, fast flight with rapid wing-beats**

colourful bill

white face

short tail

upright posture

♂ ♀

? ☑ Was its bill black with a white vertical line?

? ☑ Were its upperparts black?

? ☑ Were its underparts white?

? ☑ Did it look like an auk?

my notes

I saw this bird on (date)

....

at (time)

....

It was (activity)

....

my pictures

my observations

Razorbill *(Alca torda)*

Half the world's population of razorbills breeds in Britain and Ireland. The razorbill is ungainly on land, and walks with a shuffle, but is perfectly at home in the sea, where it is an excellent swimmer. When feeding its young, it can carry up to a dozen small fish at a time in its large beak. Razorbills start to come ashore near the breeding-site in February, but do not begin nesting and breeding until March or later. They begin to leave the site again in July. They spend the entire winter at sea, unless driven ashore by particularly strong storms. British breeding birds migrate as far as the Mediterranean in winter.

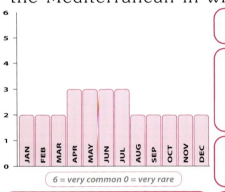

6 = very common 0 = very rare

RESIDENT/VISITOR
Resident breeder, wintering at sea as far south as the Mediterranean.

FACTS

SIZE	Length 40 cm Weight 700 g
COLOUR	MALE: Black upper body, head, bill and wings. White underparts. FEMALE: Same as male. WINTER DIFFERENCES: Chin, throat, sides of neck white. White bill-markings turn grey.
NEST	Rocky crevices, cliff ledges and among boulders. In colonies, often mixed with kittiwakes and guillemots.
CALL	A grating 'grrr' in the colony.

black bill with white vertical line

small pointed tail

white breast

♂♀

👁 QUICK IDENTIFICATION

- **Deep, square-ended black bill**
- **Short neck, stocky body**
- **White line between bill and eye**
- **Circles landing spot several times**

? ✓ Was it flying low over the water?

? ✓ Was it black above?

? ✓ Did it have a white breast, belly and throat?

? ✓ Were its legs short and grey?

I saw this bird on (date)

....

at (time)

....

It was (activity)

....

my notes

_____

_____

_____

_____

_____

my pictures

my observations

Manx Shearwater *(Puffinus puffinus)*

The Manx shearwater elegantly skims the waves, following the water contours, tipping first one way, then the other. It breeds mainly on islands off the Irish coast and the English west coast. It has a habit of congregating on the water below the breeding site at dusk, not coming ashore until after dark, possibly to avoid predators. With its effortless, gliding flight, the Manx shearwater can travel great distances to feed, sometimes as much as 300 kilometres. Its food includes fish, crustaceans and invertebrates all picked off the sea surface. It has no trouble navigating back to its nest-site, which is in a deep burrow.

6 = very common 0 = very rare

FACTS

SIZE	Length 30–38 cm Weight 440 g
COLOUR	MALE: Black upperparts. White underparts. Black wing-tips and trailing edges of wings. FEMALE: Same as male. WINTER DIFFERENCES: None.
NEST	In a burrow, up to 1.5 m long, excavated in soft earth. A small amount of dry grass bedding.
CALL	'Kookoo- kooroo'.

RESIDENT/VISITOR
A summer breeder, visiting Britain between February and October and wintering at sea.

 QUICK IDENTIFICATION

- **Alternate wing-tips almost touching waves**
- **White underwings, dark trailing edges visible in flight**
- **Contrasting upper black and lower white plumage**
- **Long, pointed, narrow wings**

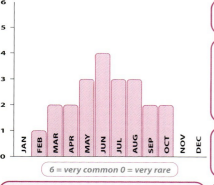

thin, short black bill

dark back

white underparts

♂ ♀

? ✓ Did it look rather goose-like?

? ✓ Did it have short, black legs?

? ✓ Was its appearance glossy black?

? ✓ Did it have impressive open wings?

I saw this bird on (date)

at (time)

It was (activity)

my notes

my pictures

my observations

Cormorant (*Phalacrocorax carbo*)

The cormorant is often seen drying its feathers, perched with wings outstretched. Its feathers become sodden when it swims, which aids the underwater pursuit of fish. It is a bird of coasts, tidal rivers and large lakes. It dives for its food, and is a strong underwater swimmer. Cormorants are often seen far inland. They fly with powerful and steady wing-beats. When it catches a fish, the cormorant brings it to the surface and shakes it vigorously before swallowing it. As well as for swimming, it uses its large webbed feet to help hatch its eggs, holding them between the tops of its feet and the warmth of its breast.

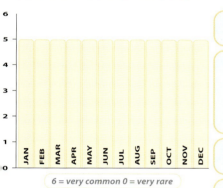

6 = very common 0 = very rare

RESIDENT/VISITOR
Resident.

👁 QUICK IDENTIFICATION

- **Long, hooked yellow bill**
- **White cheeks and chin**
- **Wide-spread wings when drying**
- **Perched on buoys and trees**

FACTS

SIZE	Length 90 cm Weight 2500 g
COLOUR	MALE: Black plumage with bronze and blue overtones. White cheeks and chin. White thigh-patches. Yellow bill. FEMALE: Same as male. WINTER DIFFERENCES: Duller; reduced white.
NEST	Twigs, seaweed and other available lining materials. On cliff ledges in colonies.
CALL	Deep croak.

white face

glossy back

white patch in summer

♂ ♀

? ✓ Did the bird have a yellow crown?

? ✓ Was it a very large, white bird with black wing-tips?

? ✓ Were its legs short and black?

? ✓ Did it fly low over the water?

I saw this bird on (date)

....

at (time)

....

It was (activity)

....

my notes

my pictures

my observations

Gannet *(Morus bassanus)*

The gannet is one of the most spectacular diving birds in northern Atlantic waters. Plummeting down from heights of up to 40 metres at speeds approaching 100 km/h, the gannet folds its wings as it approaches the water, piercing the sea surface like an arrow. It is helped in this by a lack of external nostrils which could take up water from the impact. With a wingspan of almost 2 metres, it is one of our largest sea birds. It locates its prey from a great height, especially shoals of herring and mackerel, and fishermen have often been guided to good fishing areas by the sight of diving gannets.

6
5
4
3
2
1
0

JAN FEB MAR APR MAY JUN JUL AUG SEP OCT NOV DEC

6 = very common 0 = very rare

RESIDENT/VISITOR
Resident breeder, spending non-breeding parts of year at sea, as far as the Azores.

FACTS

SIZE	Length 91 cm Weight 3000 g
COLOUR	MALE: Mainly white, with yellowish head and nape. Black primary feathers on wings; black around eyes. FEMALE: Same as male. WINTER DIFFERENCES: None.
NEST	Seaweed, earth and foliage, on rocky islands and coasts. Large colonies.
CALL	'Arrr' and 'kirra-kirra'.

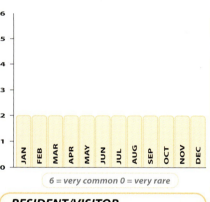

yellow crown

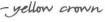

pointed white tail

♂ ♀

black wing-tips

👁 **QUICK IDENTIFICATION**
- **Large size and wingspan**
- **Spectacular plunging dive**
- **Long, spear-like bill**
- **Black 'spectacles'**

? ✓ Was it greenish black all over?

? ✓ Did it look like a cormorant?

? ✓ If seen in summer, did it have a crest?

? ✓ Were its legs grey and short?

I saw this bird on (date)

at (time)

It was (activity)

my notes

my pictures

my observations

Shag *(Phalacrocorax aristotelis)*

The shag is smaller and slimmer than its relative, the cormorant, with proportionally shorter wings and neck. It stays on wild, rocky coasts, not venturing inland. It is more at home in rough, deep waters than the cormorant, flying very close to the sea surface whatever the weather. It is a skilful and agile underwater swimmer, and feeds on shoal fish such as herrings and sand eels. It often springs entirely clear of the water before diving for fish. The shag times its breeding so that the hatchlings appear at around the same time that sand eels are most plentiful.

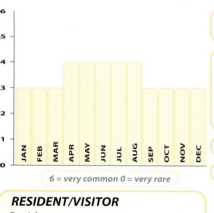

6 = very common 0 = very rare

RESIDENT/VISITOR
Resident.

FACTS

SIZE	Length 76 cm Weight 1850 g
COLOUR	MALE: Dark metallic green plumage all over. Bill black. Gape yellowish. FEMALE: Same as male. WINTER DIFFERENCES: Loses the forward-pointing crest.
NEST	Seaweed, on ledge on cliff, or in cave.
CALL	'Karr' and 'arrk-arrk'.

👁 QUICK IDENTIFICATION

- **Perches on rocks, not posts or buoys**
- **Upturned, bristly crest in spring**
- **Thinner bill than cormorant, and no facial white**
- **Dark green plumage**

crest

metallic, greenish-black plumage

black bill with yellow gape

♂♀

? ✓ Was it feeding head-down using a scything action?

? ✓ Was its bill long, curved and black?

? ✓ Did it have long, blue legs?

? ✓ Was it in a rather noisy group?

I saw this bird on (date)

....

at (time)

....

It was (activity)

....

my notes

_____

_____

_____

_____

_____

my pictures

my observations

Avocet (*Recurvirostra avosetta*)

The avocet uses its slender, upturned bill in the shallows to extract shrimps and other creatures from the mud. It sweeps its bill from side to side to dislodge them. It lives on a few estuaries in Britain, breeding on coastal lagoons in the east and south of the country. Absent from Britain for over a century due to drainage of habitats and hunting, this elegant wader returned in 1947 to East Anglia. It has successfully re-established itself due to careful management and conservation of its habitats by the Royal Society for the Protection of Birds and others.

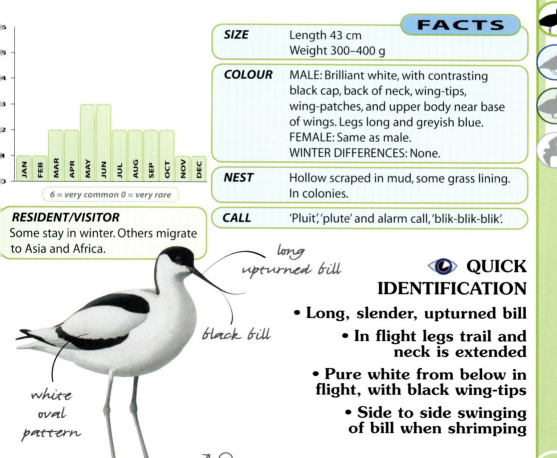

6 = very common 0 = very rare

RESIDENT/VISITOR
Some stay in winter. Others migrate to Asia and Africa.

FACTS

SIZE	Length 43 cm Weight 300–400 g
COLOUR	MALE: Brilliant white, with contrasting black cap, back of neck, wing-tips, wing-patches, and upper body near base of wings. Legs long and greyish blue. FEMALE: Same as male. WINTER DIFFERENCES: None.
NEST	Hollow scraped in mud, some grass lining. In colonies.
CALL	'Pluit', 'plute' and alarm call, 'blik-blik-blik'.

long upturned bill

black bill

white oval pattern

♂ ♀

👁 QUICK IDENTIFICATION

- **Long, slender, upturned bill**
- **In flight legs trail and neck is extended**
- **Pure white from below in flight, with black wing-tips**
- **Side to side swinging of bill when shrimping**

? ✓ Was its breast reddish-brown?

? ✓ Did it have a long, thin upturned bill with pink base?

? ✓ Was its back dappled black and chestnut?

? ✓ Were its wings grey?

I saw this bird on (date)

....

at (time)

....

It was (activity)

....

my notes

....

....

....

....

....

my pictures

my observations

Bar-tailed Godwit (*Limosa lapponica*)

Rarely seen inland, the bar-tailed godwit wades through the shallows on its long legs, probing the tidal mud and sandbanks of estuaries for food with its long bill. It is a sociable bird, which is usually seen in company with other waders, such as knots, redshanks, oystercatchers and curlews at the water's edge. The bar-tailed godwit feeds on worms, shellfish, crustaceans, water larvae and all sorts of insects. It is found in sandier areas than its relative, the black-tailed godwit, especially those rich in lugworms. When it sees the coiled worm-cast appearing on the surface, it quickly plunges its beak deep into the sand before the lugworm can burrow out of reach.

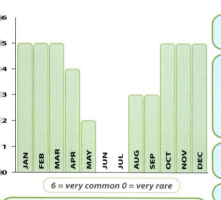

6 = very common 0 = very rare

RESIDENT/VISITOR
Winter visitor and passage migrant. Arrives on east coast between August and November. Leaves in the spring for Scandinavian and Siberian breeding-grounds.

FACTS

SIZE	Length 41 cm Weight 300 g
COLOUR	MALE: Upperparts red-brown, with black markings. Underparts rusty red, unmarked. FEMALE: Duller than male. WINTER DIFFERENCES: Loses reddish tones. Underparts pale fawn.
NEST	Hollow on ground, lined with grasses and dry leaves.
CALL	'Ved-ved-ved' in flight. Also 'kirruc-kirruc'.

long thin bill with pink base

reddish-brown breast

♂

long black legs

👁 QUICK IDENTIFICATION

- **Slightly upturned long bill**
- **No white wing-bar in flight**
- **Streaked upperparts in winter**
- **Legs do not extend far beyond tail in flight**

? ✓ Was it a large bird?

? ✓ Was its overall colour buff and brown streaks?

? ✓ Were its legs long and green?

? ✓ Did its long bill curve downwards?

I saw this bird on (date)

....

at (time)

....

It was (activity)

....

my notes

....

....

....

....

....

my pictures

Curlew (*Numenius arquata*)

The curlew disperses in the spring from its winter flocks on estuaries and shores, and moves in pairs to nesting-sites on moors, marshes and sand dunes. On the shore the curlew can often be seen with other waders, using its long, curved bill to excavate sand worms, crabs, shrimps and shellfish. Up on the moors in the breeding season, it feeds on insects and also eats plant material such as berries. The curlew is the largest of the European waders, and can sometimes be seen flying in formation with others with steady, gull-like wing beats. Its cry has an eerie, lonely quality, and can be heard at night as well as during the day.

6 = very common 0 = very rare

FACTS

SIZE	Length 50–60 cm Weight 700–1000 g
COLOUR	MALE: Head, neck and front of body, streaky brown. Back darker. Lighter underparts. White rump. FEMALE: Similar colouring, longer bill. WINTER DIFFERENCES: None.
NEST	Grass-lined hollow in field, marsh or moor.
CALL	'Curl-wee' and bubbling mating song.

RESIDENT/VISITOR
Some breed in Britain, migrating to Ireland in autumn. Others are passage migrants from Scandinavia in winter.

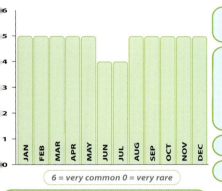

downward curved bill

buff and brown colouring

dark-green legs

♂

 **QUICK IDENTIFICATION**

- **Very long down-turned bill**
- **Distinctive call and mating song**
- **V-shaped white patch on back visible in flight**
- **Large size and long legs**

? ☑ Did it have a longish, downward curved bill?

? ☑ In winter was its overall appearance streaky black-and-white?

? ☑ In flight could you see a white V wing-bar?

? ☑ Was it quite a dumpy little bird?

I saw this bird on (date)

....

at (time)

....

It was (activity)

....

my notes

my pictures

my observations

Dunlin *(Calidris alpina)*

The dunlin visits the British Isles in huge numbers for the winter, and is the nation's commonest wader. Dunlins run and quarrel as they probe beneath the surface of estuary mud and coastal sand for snails and ragworms. The large flocks fly in close formation, and will suddenly take off from the feeding-site in unison, make a wheeling circuit, then land again to resume feeding. Those which breed in Britain arrive in April, sometimes establishing nest-sites at altitudes of up to 1000 metres in Scotland. At a distance, a close-packed flock of dunlins looks like moving smoke as they wheel and sweep over their feeding-grounds.

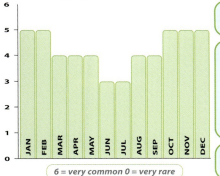

6 = very common 0 = very rare

FACTS

SIZE	Length 16–19 cm Weight 60 g
COLOUR	MALE: Upperparts brown-black with red and brown markings. Pale underparts, back and neck. Black belly and legs. FEMALE: Reddish back of neck. WINTER DIFFERENCES: Grey-brown upperparts. White and grey underparts.
NEST	Compact grass bowl, hidden in vegetation on ground.
CALL	Harsh 'treer'.

RESIDENT/VISITOR

Some are winter visitors from Scandinavia and Siberia. Some breed in far northern Britain, migrating south in winter. Passage migrants from Iceland and Greenland pass through on their way south.

QUICK IDENTIFICATION

- **Olive-black legs**
- **Fast moving feeding flocks on ground**
- **Narrow white wing-bar in flight**
- **Black belly in summer**

grey crown

black and white tail

white belly

? ✓ Was it with other birds?

? ✓ Did it have long, black legs?

? ✓ Was its overall colour grey and white in winter?

? ✓ Was it feeding on the tideline?

I saw this bird on (date)

....

at (time)

....

It was (activity)

....

my notes

my pictures

my observations

Grey Plover *(Pluvialis squatarola)*

Increasing numbers of grey plovers are spending the winter in Britain, but most go to warmer climates, travelling as far as Africa, Australasia and South America, after spending spring and summer here from April onwards. They all breed in the Siberian tundra. In Britain the grey plover is found on coastal mudflats and shores, feeding on mussels and other shellfish as well as lugworms. The grey plover rarely moves inland in Britain, preferring to stay close to the shore. It runs along the tideline on beaches, picking up insects as well as sea creatures. It usually moves in small groups, often mingling with other species, and calling noisily as it forages.

6 = very common 0 = very rare

RESIDENT/VISITOR
Winter visitor and passage migrant.

FACTS

SIZE	Length 27–30 cm Weight 200–250 g
COLOUR	MALE: White and dark grey patterned cap and back. White forehead, side of neck, breast and rump. Black face, throat and underparts. FEMALE: Same as male. WINTER DIFFERENCES: Pale throat and underparts, with grey-brown streaks. Dark grey and off-white upperparts.
NEST	Hollow in ground in Arctic tundra.
CALL	'Tlee-oo-ee'.

grey and white plumage

short, thin black bill

long black legs

♂ ♀

QUICK IDENTIFICATION

- **Black 'armpit' against white underwing in flight**
- **Jet black face and underparts framed in white in summer**
- **White wing-bar and rump visible in flight**
- **Heavy build and stout black bill**

73

? ✓ Was it a small bird?

? ✓ Was its back brown?

? ✓ Did it have a black and white head and breast?

? ✓ Was its bill orange with a black tip?

my notes

my pictures

my observations

Ringed Plover *(Charadrius hiaticula)*

The ringed plover is short and stocky, and its black facial and breast markings contrast dramatically with its white front. Together with its brown cap and back, this means it is well camouflaged against the pebbles of the shingle beaches where it often nests. The ringed plover is a stop-start feeder, running along the water's edge and stopping to bob down and capture food items on the beach, including insects, worms and crustaceans. Like other shore birds it patters the mud with its feet to bring worms to the surface. It does not probe with its bill. Some ringed plovers breed inland, alongside rivers and lakes, and also in crop fields, moving back to the coast after breeding.

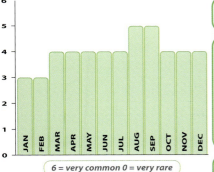

6 = very common 0 = very rare

RESIDENT/VISITOR
Both resident breeder and passage migrant.

FACTS

SIZE	Length 18–20 cm Weight 56–70 g
COLOUR	MALE: Brown crown and upperparts. White underparts. Black mask, brow-band and collar. Yellow legs. FEMALE: Breast-band and mask slightly browner than male. WINTER DIFFERENCES: White behind eye. Loses some neck and facial black.
NEST	Scraped hollow in sand, shingle or pebbles. On beaches and gravel pits.
CALL	'Too-li'.

👁 QUICK IDENTIFICATION

- **Distinctive black collar and mask**
- **Short yellow bill with black tip**
- **Prominent white upper wing-bar in flight**
- **Running and bobbing feeding movements**

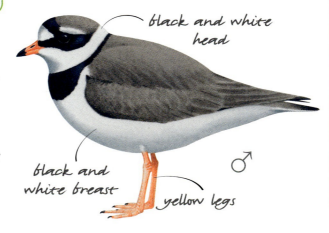

black and white head

black and white breast

♂

yellow legs

? ✓ Was it a large black-and-white bird?

? ✓ Did it have red eyes with an orange-red eye-ring?

? ✓ Were its legs pink?

? ✓ Was its bill orange?

I saw this bird on (date)
....

at (time)
....

It was (activity)
....

my notes

my pictures

my observations

Oystercatcher *(Haemaotopus ostralegus)*

The oystercatcher has a strong chisel shape at the end of its long, orange bill, which it uses to pound open tightly shut bivalves such as cockles and mussels. Everything about the oystercatcher is sturdy – bill, body and legs. It is usually seen in flocks along estuaries and seashores. It works its way energetically along the edge of the water, feeding on shellfish and worms. Outside the breeding season, huge noisy flocks of mixed resident and migrant oystercatchers assemble on shore roosts. Occasionally oystercatchers are seen among gull flocks, following tractors on agricultural land for earthworms.

6 = very common 0 = very rare

RESIDENT/VISITOR
Resident breeding populations, swelled by many winter visitors from Iceland and Scandinavia.

FACTS

SIZE	Length 40–46 cm Weight 500–600 g
COLOUR	MALE: Black head, upper breast and upperparts. White underparts. Orange-red eyes and bill. Pale pink legs. FEMALE: Same as male. WINTER DIFFERENCES: Duller, with white band across throat to sides of head.
NEST	Hollow scraped on ground in sand, grass or pebbles. Dry riverbeds.
CALL	Loud 'kleep-kleep' and alarm call, 'gleea-gleea'.

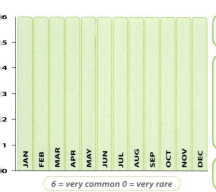

bright red eye

long orange bill

pink legs

♂ ♀

👁 QUICK IDENTIFICATION

- **Long, bright orange bill**
- **Contrasting black and white plumage**
- **White wing-bands and back in flight**
- **Sturdy pale pink legs**

? ✓ Was it a short-legged wading bird?

? ✓ Was the base of its bill yellow-orange in colour?

? ✓ Was its overall colouring black and grey?

? ✓ Were its legs yellow?

I saw this bird on (date)

....

at (time)

....

It was (activity)

....

my notes

_____

_____

_____

_____

_____

my pictures

my observations

Purple Sandpiper *(Calidris maritima)*

A small number of purple sandpipers breed in Scotland, but it is mainly a visitor to the British Isles between autumn and spring, and appears on most coasts. It is usually very tame in the presence of humans. Outside the breeding season its favourite feeding territory is the wave-splash area along rocky coasts. It forages busily in small flocks through the seaweed-covered boulders for winkles, small crabs and other tidbits, which it picks out with its shortish, slightly curving bill. Its dark winter plumage provides it with an excellent camouflage against a background of wet rocks and exposed beds of weed.

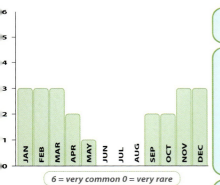

6 = very common 0 = very rare

RESIDENT/VISITOR
Winter visitor from Greenland and Scandinavia. A few pairs are resident breeders in Scotland.

FACTS

SIZE	Length 20–22 cm Weight 55–80 g
COLOUR	MALE: (Winter plumage in Britain) Very dark, slate-brown upperparts, head and breast. White belly. Spotted flanks. FEMALE: Same as male. SUMMER DIFFERENCES: (Breeding plumage in Scandinavia, Greenland) Paler, more spotted upperparts. Reddish back. Legs and bill-base more orange.
NEST	Untidy, straw, grass, feathers. Usually in a hole in trees, buildings, cliffs, nest-boxes.
CALL	'Wit', and 'weet-wit'.

QUICK IDENTIFICATION

- **Short yellow legs**
- **Yellow-orange base to bill**
- **Stocky, plump body**
- **Rock and seaweed foraging habit**

black and grey colouring

yellow-orange base to bill

yellow legs

♂ ♀

? ✓ Was it with other birds?

? ✓ Were its legs long and red?

? ✓ Was its tail short, square and black and white?

? ✓ Was the base of its bill red too?

I saw this bird on (date)

....

at (time)

....

It was (activity)

....

my notes

my pictures

my observations

Redshank (*Tringa totanus*)

The redshank breeds throughout the British Isles, nesting in marshes, moorlands and meadows. Outside the breeding season it moves to coastal flatlands and estuaries. Here it swims and wades as it probes the mud for molluscs, worms, crustaceans and insects. The redshank is a noisy bird, emitting loud alarm calls when intruders approach its nest. It does this both from perches, such as fence posts, and while flying. The male has a spectacular courting dance, approaching the female with wings raised to display the white under-surfaces, and performing a slow, high-stepping walk with his long red legs. He then begins to flutter his wings, leaving the ground entirely with each step, trilling noisily.

6 = very common 0 = very rare

RESIDENT/VISITOR
Resident breeders, plus passage migrants which visit in winter from Iceland and northern Europe.

FACTS

SIZE	Length 28 cm Weight 130 g
COLOUR	MALE: Greyish brown upperparts with dark streaks. Whitish underparts with brown markings. White trailing edge to wing. White rump. Red legs. FEMALE: Same as male. WINTER DIFFERENCES: Greyer upperparts. Whiter underparts, less spotted.
NEST	Cup-shaped, made of grass, on ground in marsh or similar. Concealed by vegetation.
CALL	'Tu-yu-yu'.

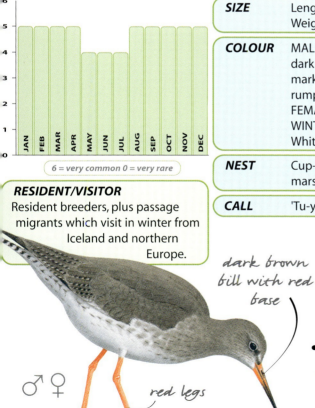

dark brown bill with red base

red legs

♂♀

👁 QUICK IDENTIFICATION

- **Bright orange-red legs**
- **Broad white trailing edge to wing**
- **Red base to bill, black tip**
- **Stands on raised perches such as posts**

? ✓ Was it a medium-sized bird?

? ✓ Did it have dark green legs?

? ✓ Was it with a lot of similar birds?

? ✓ Did it have an eye-stripe?

my notes

....

....

....

....

....

my pictures

my observations

Knot *(Calidris canutus)*

The knot is a sociable little wader. It is usually seen in large flocks on mudflats and sandy estuaries in winter in Britain, mainly on east and northwest coasts. It breeds in the Arctic regions of Europe, North America and Asia. The close-packed flocks of knots cover the feeding-ground like a moving carpet, all probing rapidly for food. Occasionally they take to the air to perform complicated formation aerobatics, all turning and wheeling at exactly the same time. A flock may contain many thousands of birds. They feed on small shellfish such as cockles and immature mussels.

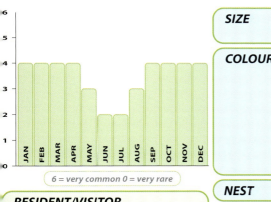

6 = very common 0 = very rare

RESIDENT/VISITOR
Winter visitor from Arctic.

FACTS

SIZE	Length 25 cm Weight 150 g
COLOUR	MALE: (Winter plumage in Britain). Pale grey-brown upperparts. Paler underparts, flecked with darker markings. FEMALE: Same as male. WINTER DIFFERENCES: (Breeding plumage in Arctic). Distinctive brick-red head and underparts. Black-brown markings on russet upperparts.
NEST	Scraped hollow in tundra lined with lichens.
CALL	'Nutt' and 'whistling 'twit-twit'.

👁 QUICK IDENTIFICATION

- **Very dense flocks wheeling in unison**
- **Pale rump, white wing-bar in flight**
- **Small, bulky bird with straight, dark bill**
- **Feeds night and day**

eye-stripe

grey back

short straight bill

dark green legs

♂ ♀

? ☑ Was it feeding in a small flock?

? ☑ Was it quite a small bird?

? ☑ Did it have a black bill and legs?

? ☑ Was it black at the bend of its wing?

my notes

_____

_____

_____

_____

_____

my pictures

my observations

Sanderling *(Calidris alba)*

T he sanderling is always on the move, usually running. On the ground the flocks run like streams of insects as the birds hurry and bustle in their continual quest for worms, shellfish and shrimps. In the air flocks fly in co-ordinated movement over mudflats. The sanderling breeds in the high Arctic regions of Canada, Greenland, Scandinavia and Siberia. It migrates in winter as far south as Australasia, though some winter much further north, including those which are seen in Britain. The sanderling likes to feed right at the edge of the water where the waves break, scurrying towards the retreating water to pick up morsels, then running back up the beach as the waves return.

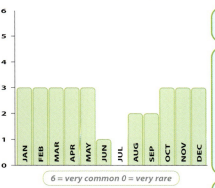

6 = very common 0 = very rare

RESIDENT/VISITOR
Winter visitor all round the coast. Passage migrant to and from Arctic. Some non-breeders stay all summer.

FACTS

SIZE	Length 20–21 cm Weight 50–60 g
COLOUR	MALE: (Winter plumage in Britain) Pale grey upperparts with faint dark markings. Dark shoulder patch. Pure white underparts. Black legs. FEMALE: Same as male. SUMMER DIFFERENCES: (Arctic breeding plumage) Head, neck and breast light chestnut. Back chestnut mottled with black.
NEST	Scrape in Arctic tundra.
CALL	'Tvik-tvik'.

👁 QUICK IDENTIFICATION

- **Large white wing-bar in flight**
- **Black bill and legs**
- **Runs as feeds close to waves**
- **Spotless white belly**

short, straight black bill

black and white tail

white breast

♂♀

? ☑ Was it a stocky bird with short, orange legs?

? ☑ Was its bill thin, short and black?

? ☑ Were its head markings quite complex?

? ☑ Was it turning stones for food?

I saw this bird on (date)

....

at (time)

....

It was (activity)

....

my notes

my pictures

my observations

Turnstone *(Arenaria interpres)*

The turnstones wintering in Britain have bred in Canada and Greenland. The passage migrants passing through Britain in spring and autumn breed in Scandinavia and winter in Africa. The turnstone has earned its name from the way it overturns stones, moves seaweed and digs sand to catch the tiny creatures which scatter as they are exposed. Rocky coasts provide it with abundant supplies of winkles, mussels and limpets, as well as the fast-moving invertebrates flushed out from beneath stones and seaweed patches. Sometimes several turnstones co-operate to overturn a heavy stone which one bird cannot manage alone.

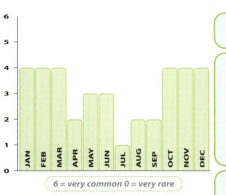

| JAN | FEB | MAR | APR | MAY | JUN | JUL | AUG | SEP | OCT | NOV | DEC |

6 = very common 0 = very rare

RESIDENT/VISITOR
Winter visitor, and spring/autumn passage migrant.

FACTS

SIZE	Length 21-25 cm Weight 80-150 g
COLOUR	MALE: (Winter plumage in Britain). Dull brown upperparts. White underparts. Dark grey bib. FEMALE: Duller than male. WINTER DIFFERENCES: (Arctic breeding plumage). Chestnut and black upperparts. Black bands on white face and neck.
NEST	On ground on rocky terrain and coastal islands.
CALL	'Tuk-a-tuk' and 'kyug'.

👁 QUICK IDENTIFICATION

- **Stone-turning activity**
- **Short-billed and stocky**
- **White and black wing**
- **White undersides and dark 'bib'**

chestnut and black colouring

white throat

orange legs

♂

? ☑ Did it have a black and yellow face?

? ☑ Could you see black 'horns' on its head?

? ☑ Was it a small bird?

? ☑ Was it part of a small flock?

I saw this bird on (date)
....

at (time)
....

It was (activity)
....

my notes

_____

_____

_____

_____

_____

my pictures

Shore Lark *(Eremophila alpestris)*

A rare winter visitor, the shore lark usually turns up on Britain's eastern and southeastern coasts in late autumn. There it can find the shingle, sand and salt marshes which are its preferred winter habitat, after breeding in the dry tundras of northern Scandinavia. Some shore larks stay in Britain for the winter, but others are passing through, and cross to the Continent as winter deepens. The shore lark is a sociable bird, sometimes seen in company with snow buntings and Lapland buntings. Its winter and summer diets are completely different. It lives on seeds, buds and insects when breeding, then switches to shellfish and crustaceans from the water's edge in winter.

FACTS

SIZE	Length 16.5 cm Weight 36 g
COLOUR	MALE: Yellow head. Black feather 'horns'. Black eye and cheek markings. Upperparts brown. Underparts white. Wide black 'bib'. FEMALE: Not so much black. No horns. WINTER DIFFERENCES: Duller.
NEST	On ground. Grass stalks, lined with hair and plant down.
CALL	'Tsee'. In flight 'tsee-di-diu'. Warbling song.

Chart (vertical axis 0–6): JAN, FEB, MAR, APR, MAY, JUN, JUL, AUG, SEP, OCT, NOV, DEC

6 = very common 0 = very rare

RESIDENT/VISITOR
Winter visitor and passage migrant. Occasional breeding pairs in Scotland.

QUICK IDENTIFICATION

- **Black feather 'horns' of male**
- **Wave-like flight**
- **Yellowish head and black mask**
- **Longish tail with white outer feathers**

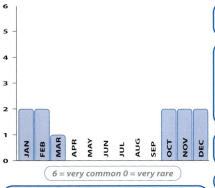

horns

black crest

short black legs

89

? ☑ Did it have a black tail with grey outer feathers?

? ☑ Was it streaky grey and brown in colour?

? ☑ Did it have a faint eyebrow?

? ☑ Was its call harsh but clear?

my notes

my pictures

my observations

Rock Pipit (Anthus petrosus)

Rock pipits are hard to see as they forage among coastal rocks and seaweed, feeding on tiny molluscs. Their dark colouring is a good camouflage among the rocks and vegetation, and they are often only noticed when they take to their wings, flitting erratically between rocks and along the shore. The rock pipit's calls and song are particularly loud, as it has to compete with the general noise of waves crashing on a rocky shore. In winter it may extend its food searches to estuaries and mudflats, and sometimes appears at inland reservoirs. Rock pipits are found around most of the coastline except for stretches without rocky shores.

6 = very common 0 = very rare

FACTS

SIZE	Length 16 cm Weight 21–30 g
COLOUR	MALE: Dark greyish brown upperparts. Buff underparts. Speckled throat and breast. Pale line through eye. Dark legs. Grey outer tail feathers. FEMALE: Same as male. WINTER DIFFERENCES: None.
NEST	Grass, hair, seaweed, in rocky crevice, or concealed in shore vegetation.
CALL	'Peep-peep' alarm call.

RESIDENT/VISITOR
Resident breeders, with some Scandinavian migrants.

QUICK IDENTIFICATION

- **Often seen perched on rocks**
- **Forages at sea level among rocks and weed**
- **Repeats alarm call, flying upwards**
- **Combination of dark upperparts and dark legs**

streaky patterning

black tail with grey outer feathers

dark legs

♂♀

91

? Was the bird with others?

? Did it have a black-and-white tail?

? Was its bill black and stubby?

? Was a lot of the bird white?

I saw this bird on (date)
....

at (time)
....

It was (activity)
....

my notes

_____

_____

_____

_____

_____

my pictures

my observations

Snow Bunting *(Plectrophenax nivalis)*

The snow bunting is a bird of rocks, from the rocky tops of northern mountains, to the rocky shores of Scotland and eastern England. In winter it appears along North Sea coasts in flocks. Snow buntings call noisily as they feed on seeds and insects. The flock moves across the ground in a series of running, pecking and fluttering movements. Because of the large amount of white in their plumage, snow buntings are sometimes known locally as snowflakes. A small number of snow buntings may now be regular breeders in the Cairngorm mountains and other Scottish ranges, but most are winter visitors.

6 = very common 0 = very rare

RESIDENT/VISITOR
Winter visitor, rarely breeding in Scottish mountains.

FACTS

SIZE	Length 16.5 cm Weight 30–40 g
COLOUR	MALE: (Winter plumage in Britain) Rusty buff head and throat band. Brown upperparts with dark streaks. Underparts creamy, white wing-patches. FEMALE: Wing-patches smaller than in male. SUMMER DIFFERENCES: (Arctic breeding plumage) Male – white head and body, contrasting black on wings. Female – grey upperparts, off-white underparts.
NEST	Grass, moss, feathers, in rocky crevice.
CALL	'Brrr' and 'tsrrr'. Trilling song.

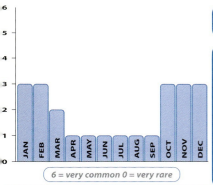

white on wing

stubby bill

♂

👁 QUICK IDENTIFICATION

- **Bouncy, wave-like flight**
- **White in wings and tail visible in flight**
- **Breeding male stark black and white contrasts**
- **Rusty head colouring in winter**

? Was it an all-black bird?

? Were its legs grey?

? Did it have a yellow bill?

? Was it with other ducks?

I saw this bird on (date)

....

at (time)

....

It was (activity)

....

my notes

my pictures

my observations

Common Scoter *(Melanitta nigra)*

The male common scoter is the only duck with totally black plumage. Common scoters breed on lakes and pools in the Arctic tundra, and move to sea coasts in winter. They feed by diving for molluscs, especially mussels. A few pairs breed on lakes in Scotland, but most common scoters that appear in British waters are winter visitors seen swimming and feeding off the coast. They are often in the company of velvet scoters. The common scoter spends most of its time at sea, and is capable of diving to great depths, and stays under water for up to a minute at a time.

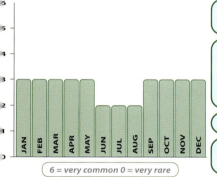

6 = very common 0 = very rare

FACTS

SIZE	Length 45–55 cm Weight 700–1400 g
COLOUR	MALE: All-black. Yellow on upper bill. FEMALE: Chocolate-brown. Paler cheeks and neck. Black bill. WINTER DIFFERENCES: None.
NEST	Concealed on ground, near water.
CALL	Male – low piping call. Female – grating call.

RESIDENT/VISITOR
Winter visitor from Arctic. A few resident breeders in Scotland.

◉ QUICK IDENTIFICATION

- **Totally black male**
- **Pale cheeks of female**
- **Dense sea flocks. Frequent diving**
- **No white in male or female plumage**

yellow bill with black knob at base

all-black plumage

♂

? Was it mainly black all over?

? Did it have red legs?

? Was its bill yellow?

? Did it have a white wing-patch?

I saw this bird on (date)

....

at (time)

....

It was (activity)

....

my notes

my pictures

my observations

Velvet Scoter *(Melanitta fusca)*

The velvet scoter visits the British Isles in winter. It is bigger and heavier than its relative, the common scoter. It is often seen close to the shore. Velvet scoters tend to be seen in small flocks, sometimes mixed in with common scoters. On land the velvet scoter is awkward, and rarely comes ashore in Britain. It is an accomplished swimmer and diver, reaching depths of up to 20 metres. It has been timed under water at up to three minutes. It feeds on molluscs and crustaceans when at sea, but during its Arctic breeding season includes roots and water plants in its diet.

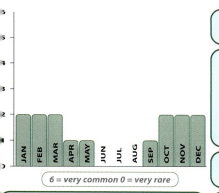

6 = very common 0 = very rare

RESIDENT/VISITOR
Winter visitor and passage migrant to east coasts of Scotland and England from Scandinavia and Siberia.

FACTS

SIZE	Length 51–58 cm Weight 1200–1800 g
COLOUR	MALE: Overall black with white eye-patches, yellow-red bill and red legs. White wing-patches. FEMALE: Dark brown. Pale head-patches. Black bill. WINTER DIFFERENCES: None.
NEST	On ground, grass lined with down, near lakes on tundra and moorland.
CALL	Male, piping call, 'kyu'. Female hoarse, churring 'braaa'.

QUICK IDENTIFICATION

- **White wing-patches visible in flight**
- **Pale head-patches of female**
- **White eye-patches and yellow upper bill of male**
- **Red legs and feet**

large yellow bill

white eye-patch

white wing-patch

♂

? ✓ Did it have a flat forehead?

? ✓ Was its breast tinged with pink?

? ✓ Were its legs short and brown?

? ✓ Was its back white?

I saw this bird on (date)

....

at (time)

....

It was (activity)

....

my notes

my pictures

my observations

Eider (*Somateria mollissima*)

Famous for the heat-retaining qualities of its down, the eider duck is most commonly seen in the British Isles in Scottish coastal waters. It is a resident breeder, with increasing numbers of breeding pairs in both Scotland and Ireland. Eiders dive for molluscs, often at low tide, when inshore waters are shallower. From time to time they come out of the water to rest on rocks and islets. The female eider sometimes goes without food for two or three weeks while sitting on the eggs. After hatching, the ducklings are often looked after by one or more aunties, who oversee several broods.

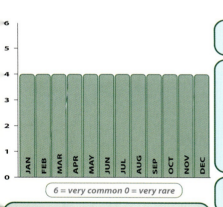

6 = very common 0 = very rare

RESIDENT/VISITOR
Resident breeder and winter visitor.

FACTS

SIZE	Length 50–71 cm Weight 1500–2800 g
COLOUR	MALE: Black crown. White head, neck and breast. Green markings on back of head and upper bill. Rosy flush on breast. Black underparts. FEMALE: Reddish brown upperparts. Pale brown underparts, barred with dark grey. WINTER DIFFERENCES: None.
NEST	Grass, seaweed, down, on ground in the open, or in a rocky crevice.
CALL	Male 'uhuu-uhuu'. Female 'korr-korr'.

QUICK IDENTIFICATION

- **White breast and back, black underparts (male)**
- **Feathers coming down to peak over bill**
- **Green markings on head (male)**
- **Wedge-shaped bill and head**

white back

pink tinge to breast

short brown legs

♂

? ☑ Was its tail long and pointed?

? ☑ Did it have bold black and white markings?

? ☑ Did it have short, black legs?

? ☑ Was its head large?

I saw this bird on (date)

....

at (time)

....

It was (activity)

....

my notes

_____

_____

_____

_____

_____

my pictures

Long-tailed Duck (*Clangula hyemalis*)

The long-tailed duck is a winter visitor. It is seen most commonly between northeast England and the Shetland Islands, and in the Outer Hebrides. A large proportion – up to 75 per cent – of the British winter population lives around the waters and inlets of the Moray Firth. The long-tailed duck breeds in northern tundra lands, moving south to winter on the sea. It dives for its food of molluscs and crustaceans, and prefers to spend its winter break in shallow waters. It is a fast flier, and has no fear of harsh weather conditions, swimming and diving however rough the sea.

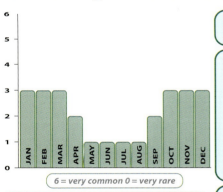

6 = very common 0 = very rare

RESIDENT/VISITOR
Winter visitor.

FACTS

SIZE	Length 40–53 cm Weight 600–800 g
COLOUR	MALE: (Winter plumage in Britain) White all over, with dark cheek-patch. Black markings on back and wings. Long black tail. Pink band across black bill. FEMALE: Duller and browner than male. No long tail. Grey ear-patch. SUMMER DIFFERENCES: (Arctic breeding plumage) Male – dark brown upperparts.
NEST	On ground in tundra on lake islands.
CALL	'Calloo'.

QUICK IDENTIFICATION

- **Unique long tail of male**
- **Wings dark top and bottom in flight**
- **Dark bill with pink band (male)**
- **Dark circular cheek-patch (male)**

pink bill

black and white markings

long pointed tail

♂

? Was the duck a slim shape?

? Did it have a dark green head with a double crest?

? Were its legs and bill red?

? Was its tail short and grey?

I saw this bird on (date)

....

at (time)

....

It was (activity)

....

my notes

_____

_____

_____

_____

_____

my pictures

Red-breasted Merganser *(Mergus serrator)*

The red-breasted merganser is a bird of inlets, shallow coastal waters, inland lakes and rivers. It is a resident breeder in Ireland and Scotland, with some pairs in northwest England and Wales. It is a saw-billed duck, so named because it has a serrated edge to its beak, which helps it keep a grip on fish caught under water. It flies low and fast over the water surface, and is often to be seen swimming along with its head submerged as it scans for fish. After diving and catching a fish, the red-breasted merganser brings it to the surface to swallow it, then performs a wing-flapping display, followed by a drink of sea water.

6 = very common 0 = very rare

(Bar chart: JAN, FEB, MAR, APR, MAY, JUN, JUL, AUG, SEP, OCT, NOV, DEC — all bars at level 3)

RESIDENT/VISITOR
Resident breeder. Some Scandinavian winter visitors.

FACTS

SIZE	Length 52–58 cm Weight 900–1200 g
COLOUR	MALE: Green-black head with crest. Spotted chestnut breast. Grey flanks. White underparts and collar. Red bill. FEMALE: Grey body. Chestnut head and crest merging into neck. White wing-patches. WINTER DIFFERENCES: Male plumage similar to female.
NEST	Grass, leaves and down, on ground. Hidden among plants and boulders.
CALL	Male 'yiuv' and 'orr'. Female 'rok-rok-rok'.

👁 QUICK IDENTIFICATION

- **Double-pointed crest**
- **Slender scarlet bill**
- **Orange-brown breast, spotted (male)**
- **White neck collar (male)**

red bill

double crest

speckled breast

♂

? ☑ Was it a large bird?

? ☑ Did it have a rusty coloured band on its breast?

? ☑ Were its head and neck dark green?

? ☑ Were its legs pink?

I saw this bird on (date)

....

at (time)

....

It was (activity)

....

my notes

_____

_____

_____

_____

_____

my pictures

my observations

Shelduck (*Tadorna tadorna*)

The colourful shelduck pairs up with its mate for more than one season. The pair establishes separate nesting and feeding territories, often a considerable distance apart. The female shelduck chooses a burrow in which to lay her eggs. When the young are hatched the parents escort them on what can be a long walk to the water where they can feed. They travel in single file, with one parent leading, and the other bringing up the rear. The shelduck is the largest duck in the British Isles, feeding mainly on muddy estuaries and sandy shores. Its broad bill acts as a sieve for separating molluscs from mud.

6 = very common 0 = very rare

RESIDENT/VISITOR
Resident breeder.

FACTS

SIZE	Length 60–70 cm Weight 800–1400 g
COLOUR	MALE: Brilliant white body and wings. Green-black head and neck, base of wings, rear underside. Wide rust band around body and breast. Green and rust patches to rear of wings. Black wing-tips. Coral-red bill with knob. FEMALE: Duller than male. White facial marks. No knob on bill. WINTER DIFFERENCES: Duller.
NEST	Down-lined, in burrow or hole in tree.
CALL	Male, low whistle, 'huee'. Female, deep rapid quacks, 'ak-ak-ak'.

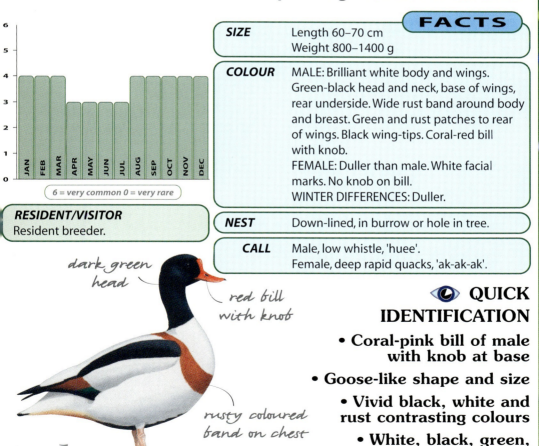

dark green head

red bill with knob

rusty coloured band on chest

♂

👁 QUICK IDENTIFICATION

- **Coral-pink bill of male with knob at base**

- **Goose-like shape and size**

- **Vivid black, white and rust contrasting colours**

- **White, black, green, rust wings in flight**

? Did it have a dark head and white neck flash?
☑

? Was its rump white?
☑

? Did it have a black throat?
☑

? Was its crown black?
☑

I saw this bird on (date)

....

at (time)

....

It was (activity)

....

my notes

_____

_____

_____

_____

_____

my pictures

my observations

Brent Goose *(Branta bernicla)*

The brent goose eats plant food for the most part, feeding on eel grass, algae and marsh plants in the salt marshes and muddy estuaries where it grazes. It also eats young cereal plants, and picks up the fallen grain from stubble after harvesting. Like most geese it enjoys company, and feeds, flies and roosts in close-packed flocks. There are two branches of the brent goose family. The dark-bellied birds fly to southern British estuaries from Russia. The pale-bellied birds fly from Greenland to Ireland, and from Spitzbergen to northeast England. The brent goose is the smallest of the European geese.

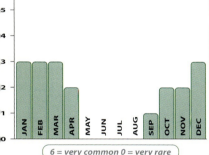

6 = very common 0 = very rare

RESIDENT/VISITOR
Winter visitor from Arctic.

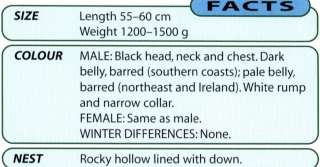

FACTS

SIZE	Length 55–60 cm Weight 1200–1500 g
COLOUR	MALE: Black head, neck and chest. Dark belly, barred (southern coasts); pale belly, barred (northeast and Ireland). White rump and narrow collar. FEMALE: Same as male. WINTER DIFFERENCES: None.
NEST	Rocky hollow lined with down.
CALL	'Rronk-rronk'.

QUICK IDENTIFICATION

- **Black head and neck**
- **Narrow white collar**
- **Small size for a goose**
- **White rump distinctive in flight**

white neck-flash

white rump

dark belly

♂ ♀

? ☑ Was its head a dark glossy green?

? ☑ Was its belly white?

? ☑ Was its bill large and grey?

? ☑ Did it have a short, black tail?

I saw this bird on (date)

....

at (time)

....

It was (activity)

....

my notes

_____

_____

_____

_____

_____

my pictures

my observations

Scaup (Aythya marila)

The scaup is a champion diver and swimmer, which feeds in the roughest seas. It can dive for half a minute at a time to depths of around 4 metres for shellfish and worms. On occasion it can stay under water for a minute, and reach depths of 7 metres. Many of the scaups overwintering around British shores are visitors from Iceland and Scandinavia, where they breed in colonies on islets in lakes and tundra pools. The scaup likes to congregate with other diving ducks. Its numbers have decreased dramatically in certain areas since the reduction of the waste grain that was once dumped by Scottish brewers and distillers, and which attracted huge scaup flocks.

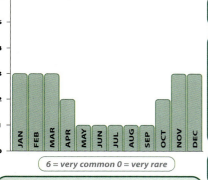

6 = very common 0 = very rare

RESIDENT/VISITOR
Winter visitor from Iceland, and passage migrant.

FACTS

SIZE	Length 42-51 cm Weight 900-1200 g
COLOUR	MALE: Green-black head. Black breast and tail. Pale grey back. White underparts. FEMALE: Chestnut head and breast. Pale grey back. Pale brown barred underparts. Conspicuous white patch at base of bill. WINTER DIFFERENCES: Male is paler, with brown barred back and underparts.
NEST	Feather and down-lined hollow near water.
CALL	Male, soft cooing courting voice. Female, 'karr-karr'.

glossy, dark green head

grey back

white belly

♂

QUICK IDENTIFICATION

- **Narrow black tip to bill**
- **Female – bold white area round bill base**
- **Female – grey back**
- **Male – green-black head, no crest**

? ✓ Was it a small bird?

? ✓ Was it all black with a white rump?

? ✓ Was its tail square-shaped?

? ✓ Were its wings brown and rounded?

I saw this bird on (date)

....

at (time)

....

It was (activity)

....

my notes

my pictures

my observations

Storm Petrel *(Hydrobates pelagicus)*

The storm petrel, no larger than a sparrow, stays at sea most of its life. It survives the stormiest weather despite its small size. Storm petrels have learned to follow ships, fluttering over the wake to pick up scraps. Their natural food is plankton, tiny animal and plant organisms which they harvest from the sea surface. In its breeding season the storm petrel goes ashore after dark to its breeding-sites on islands on the western coasts of Scotland and Ireland, and on the Northern Isles. Sailors once called storm petrels Mother Carey's chickens, and thought that large numbers of them foretold approaching bad weather.

6 = very common 0 = very rare

RESIDENT/VISITOR
Resident breeder.

FACTS

SIZE	Length 14–18 cm Weight 25 g
COLOUR	MALE: Sooty black all over, apart from white rump and pale underwing bar. FEMALE: Same as male. WINTER DIFFERENCES: None.
NEST	In burrows and rocky crevices on islands around Ireland, Scotland and as far north as Iceland.
CALL	Purring voice in its burrow.

👁 QUICK IDENTIFICATION

- **Small size and bat-like fluttering flight**
- **Feet pattering on sea surface**
- **Square-ended tail**
- **White rump contrasts with black plumage**

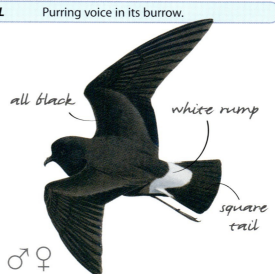

all black

white rump

square tail

♂ ♀

INDEX

Cover photograph of Puffins by Kevin Schafer/CORBIS